renewed Jan 2016

D0258909

HODDER
20TH CENTURY
HISTORY

THE GREAT WAR

SECOND EDITION

This book is to be returned on or before the last date stamped below.

11/10/04

CONTENTS

Key Issues

- Why did war break out in 1914?
- Why did men volunteer to fight it?

The simple answer to why war broke out in 1914 is that none of the great powers tried that hard to avoid it. Tension between the leading powers in Europe had existed for over two decades and gradually two alliance groups had come into existence.

Britain, France and Russia formed alliances or agreements with each other because they all shared a common fear. They all felt threatened by Germany. France felt threatened by Germany's large army. This fear was mixed with a desire for revenge because the Germans had seized two French provinces, Alsace and Lorraine, on the French–German border in a war in 1871.

Britain had become anxious about the growth of Germany's navy. The British feared it could be used in a war to cut Britain off from its Empire and vital supplies. Russia's worry was more to do with Germany's ally, Austria. Russia and Austria competed against each other for influence in the Balkans region of south-east Europe.

THE ALLIANCE SYSTEM

By 1914 two strong alliance systems were in place. The Entente Powers of Britain, France and Russia faced the Central Powers of Germany and Austria. In June 1914 the war was triggered off by the assassination of the heir to the throne of the Austrian Empire. The Austrian government blamed Serbia and declared war on Serbia on 28 July 1914. At this point the various alliance agreements kicked in. Germany came into the war in support of Austria, and Russia came to the assistance of Serbia. Within a week, Britain and France were also at war with the Central Powers.

WHY DID MEN VOLUNTEER?

During August and September 1914, 736,000 Britons volunteered for the British army. By 1916 2.5 million had done so. Their reasons varied. Most went to fight out of a sense of **patriotism**, honour and duty. They believed that it was their duty to fight for their country and that it was a matter of honour.

The alliance system in Europe in 1914.

Germany and her allies

Britain and her allies

Joined war on Germany's side (year in brackets)

Joined war on Britain's side (year in brackets)

A SOURCE

Cheering crowds on 3 August 1914, outside Buckingham Palace where the King and Queen appeared on the balcony. It had just been announced that Britain was preparing for war.

Britain and its Empire seemed to be threatened by the 'beastly Huns', as the Germans were often described in the **propaganda** of the time.

Not all men enlisted for honour or duty. To the unemployed, even the average army pay of nine or ten shillings a week was better than nothing and encouraged some to join up – though it didn't compare very well with Australian troops who were paid six shillings a day. A weekly pay of ten shillings was about a third of what an unskilled worker earned but only a little less than an apprentice.

B SOURCE

The historian, Denis Winter, describes the reasons some men volunteered for the army in *Death's Men*, 1979.

Bert Warrant joined the 10th Londons after robbing the Hackney Empire [a cinema] of £300. Private Jenkins took similar evasive action from police in hot pursuit after he had looted German shops in Billingsgate. Men arrested after the lootings of 17 October 1914 in Deptford High Street, which were aimed at German shops, were given the choice of 18 months' hard labour or immediate join-up.

C SOURCE

Government poster issued in the early years of the war.

Come into the ranks and fight for your King and Country–Don't stay in the crowd and stare

YOU ARE WANTED AT·THE·FRONT

ENLIST TO·DAY

PALS' BATTALIONS

The glamour of a uniform and the chance for adventure attracted a good number of young men – especially since everybody expected the war to be over by the Christmas of 1914. In the meantime, men who volunteered together were promised that they could fight together in what became known as the 'Pals' battalions'. Men from the same towns or cities formed regiments like the 'Sheffield Pals' or the 'Barnsley Pals'. Former pupils at private schools also formed their own battalions. These regiments had tremendous morale because they knew each other or came from the same area.

Peer group pressure was hard to resist. If all your workmates were joining up, it was easier to go along with the crowd. It took courage to resist this. It took even more courage when men out of uniform were handed white feathers by women as a sign of their 'cowardice'. If you weren't in uniform you could find it hard to get served in pubs. For one reason or another, it seemed a lot simpler to sign up for a war which would be 'over by Christmas' anyway.

D SOURCE

One veteran, Robert Burns, remembering why he volunteered for the British army in 1914 in an interview in the 1990s (from *Veterans*, Richard van Emden and Steve Humphries, 1998).

*I think it was excitement more than anything that made me join up. I was too young to understand what **patriotism** really was. I lived in the country and there were not many boys my age, so I thought it would be nice to be with a lot of lads on something of a picnic, because we all thought the war would be over by Christmas.*

Questions

a **What does Source B tell us about the sort of men who volunteered to fight in 1914?**

b **Use Source C and your own knowledge to explain why men volunteered for the army in the early years of the war.**

c **How useful is Source A as evidence of the British public's reaction to the outbreak of war? Use Source A and your own knowledge to answer this question.**

d **Is Source D a fair interpretation of why men volunteered for the army in the First World War? Use Source D and your own knowledge to answer this question.**

Key Issue

Why were some men unwilling to fight?

Men clearly had many different reasons for supporting the war – **patriotism**, duty, a sense of adventure, a chance to escape poverty or even prison. But there was also a tiny minority who opposed the war because of their personal beliefs. In January 1916 the government introduced **conscription**. This meant that most single, fit men aged between 18 and 41 now had to serve in one of the armed services. In March 1916 this was extended to married men as well. Conscription was necessary because not enough men were volunteering. In December 1915 only 55,000 volunteered, compared with 436,000 in September 1914.

The **Military Service** Act of January 1916 excused from service men in essential or 'reserved' occupations, such as miners, shipyard workers, and 'those who could show a conscientious objection'. Tribunals were set up to hear the cases of conscientious objectors (COs). These were men who would not fight on the grounds of conscience. 16,000 men were registered as COs.

PACIFISTS AND SOCIALISTS

COs gave a variety of different reasons. Some objected to the war because of their religious views: they were **pacifist** Christians, like Quakers, and opposed violence in all circumstances. Others were not pacifists but objected to this war in particular. These men were **socialists** and refused to kill their fellow workers, whether they were Germans or not. They believed the war was being fought to make money for the wealthy factory owners.

The vast majority of these COs agreed to do some kind of service which was helpful to the war effort but which would keep them out of combat. Some became stretcher bearers or worked on farms. A small minority, about 1500 men, refused to do even this. They were **absolutists** and refused to do anything which would help the war. They argued that agreeing to do farmwork, for example, simply allowed another man to fight and pull the trigger in their place. These absolutists were sent to do hard

labour in prison. Some were put under control of the army and harshly treated, but not all soldiers hated them (see Source D). When the war ended, the authorities kept them in prison for another six months so that the returning troops would get whatever jobs were going. They were also stopped from voting in elections until 1926.

BUSINESS REASONS

Some men were unwilling to fight for more practical reasons than those of COs. It is possible that the most enthusiastic volunteers for the war were either the very rich or the poor. The privileged upper classes of England were as patriotic as any group but they also had employees to look after their estates and concerns while they were away. The very poor had no businesses to worry about and often not even a job to leave. But the self-employed or people who ran small businesses faced real problems if they or their employees enlisted. What would happen to their businesses (see Source B)?

This Australian poster suggests that men who avoided the war were taking the coward's way out.

SLACKERS OR COWARDS?

On average, about four in every five men who appeared before a tribunal had their claim accepted. Not all those who appeared before tribunals, though, had convincing excuses. The man who said he should be excused war service because he had to bring his wife tea in bed every morning had his appeal turned down!

In 1916 Britain was fighting a desperate war against a powerful enemy. No one knew who would win but everyone knew just how many lives the war had already cost. In these circumstances, the government deserves credit for allowing the principle that some men had good reasons not to fight. Conscientious objectors or those who avoided joining up when it was still voluntary were very unpopular with the public. Some criticised the government for allowing 'cowards' or 'slackers' to get out of doing their duty. Source C shows one view of those men who weren't prepared to join up.

A SOURCE

James Maxton was a member of a British socialist party. The letters 'G R' in the last line stand for *Gregorius Rex* or King George in Latin. Lord Derby was in charge of recruiting volunteers for the British army. (from *The Pity of War*, Niall Ferguson, 1998).

Oh, I'm Henry Dubb
And I won't go to war
Because I don't know
What they are all fighting for

To Hell with the Kaiser
To Hell with the Tsar
To Hell with Lord Derby
And also G R.

B SOURCE

This application to avoid **military service** was made in September 1918 by a wine shop owner to keep his employee, Douglas Merry, out of the army (from a document in the Public Record Office).

Mr. Merry is the only man of my original staff left, the others having joined without appeal. He is in charge of my branch at Church End, Finchley, and is taking the place of my own son who is serving [in the armed forces] and is really now my only responsible employee, I respectfully apply for his further exemption [from military service].

Since August 1914 he has been serving as a Special Constable in addition to which he is doing Fire Brigade work.

C SOURCE

A cartoon from a popular British magazine, *Punch*, in 1914. The man is saying, after reading the headlines on the poster, 'Great Scott! I must do something. Dashed if don't get some more flags for the jigger [motor bike]!'

"GREAT SCOTT! I MUST DO SOMETHING. DASHED IF I DON'T GET SOME MORE FLAGS FOR THE OLD JIGGER!"

D SOURCE

A British solider describing his attitude to absolutist opponents of the war (from *Forgotten Voices of the Great War*, M Arthur, 2002).

Ever since then, I've admired these men intensely. I would take my hat off to them any time because I realise that . . . they had far more guts than we did who were doing these things to them.

Questions

a What does Source A tell us about James Maxton's attitude to the war and the people in power?

b Use Source B and your own knowledge to explain why some men tried to avoid military service.

c How useful is Source C in explaining the attitude of the British people to men who didn't enlist? Use Source C and your own knowledge to answer this question.

d Is Source D a fair interpretation of the attitude of people to absolutist opponents of the war? Use Source D and your own knowledge to answer the question.

Key Issue

- How did the government portray the Germans?

PROPAGANDA

Before the introduction of **conscription** in January 1916 the government relied on volunteers for its armed forces. It used various **propaganda** techniques to encourage men to enlist. Propaganda involves the use of ideas to persuade people to believe certain things or behave in a certain way. Sometimes propaganda involves the use of deliberate lies to achieve this effect. The British government during the Great War certainly made little effort to check the truth of its stories when it published reports about German 'atrocities' – as the Bryce Commission affair makes clear.

THE BRYCE COMMISSION

Stories of the atrocities committed by the Germans against 'gallant little Belgium' led many to enlist. A report by Lord Bryce (May 1915) into these 'atrocities' was translated into 30 languages. The report told of the rape of 20 Belgian girls in public at Liege and of how a soldier had bayoneted a two-year-old child (see Source C). Another German soldier had sliced off the breasts of a peasant girl. But Bryce's committee did not interview a single witness to these events. The reports were supposed to be based on 1200 statements taken from Belgian refugees in Britain but no trace of these interviews has ever been found.

A Belgian investigation in 1922 could find no evidence to support these claims either. By then, of course, the Bryce Commission report had achieved its purpose in stoking up hatred against the Germans. However, clearly some 5000 Belgian civilians did die during the German advance into Belgium. Many were shot by the Germans as reprisals for attacks on their troops or simply killed as the result of the fighting.

CENSORSHIP

Preventing the population from learning of bad news is another way of controlling and shaping people's attitudes. Newspaper and radio reports were heavily censored to keep details of defeats from the public. News of the disaster at Gallipoli (see Chapter 9) was censored and would have stayed that way until after the war, if it hadn't been for the actions of an Australian journalist called Keith Murdoch. Murdoch was arrested and his story confiscated but it still got out. The news led to the dismissal of the commander of the Gallipoli forces.

The military authorities claimed that such news was bad for public morale and that it should be censored. Others argued that **censorship** was more about protecting the image and reputation of the army leaders than the national interest.

A SOURCE

A British propaganda poster showing ill-treatment of British wounded by the Germans.

RED CROSS OR IRON CROSS?

WOUNDED AND A PRISONER
OUR SOLDIER CRIES FOR WATER.

THE GERMAN "SISTER"
POURS IT ON THE GROUND BEFORE HIS EYES.

THERE IS NO WOMAN IN BRITAIN
WHO WOULD DO IT.

THERE IS NO WOMAN IN BRITAIN
WHO WILL FORGET IT.

THE CHURCH

The Church of England was keen to give its support to the war effort. Sometimes this support was a little over the top. One clergyman claimed that the Germans planned to kill every British male child if they won the war. Some bishops, though, in 1917 reminded Christians that it was their duty to love their enemies – even Germans. They were attacked for undermining morale.

B SOURCE

A British poster from 1918 to persuade people to lend money to the government by warning them what Britain would be like if Germany won.

C SOURCE

The Bryce Commission Report included this eyewitness account by a Belgian woman of the murder of a Belgian child by a German soldier. A bayonet was a long knife, about 43 cms long, which was attached to the end of a rifle for stabbing the enemy.

One day when the Germans were not actually bombarding the town I left my house to go to my mother's house in High Street. My husband was with me. I saw eight German soldiers, and they were drunk. They were singing and making a lot of noise and dancing about. As the German soldiers came along the street I saw a small child, whether boy or girl I could not see, come out of a house. The child was about two years of age. The child came into the middle of the street so as to be in the way of the soldiers. The soldiers were walking in twos. The first line of two passed the child; one of the second line, the man on the left, stepped aside and drove his bayonet with both hands into the child's stomach lifting the child into the air on his bayonet and carrying it away on his bayonet, he and his comrades still singing. The child screamed when the soldier struck it with his bayonet, but not afterwards.

D SOURCE

Until 1916 the British government tried through posters and other propaganda to persuade Englishmen to enlist by appealing to their pride or their sense of duty (from *The Poster in History*, M Gallo, 1989).

Questions

a What does Source A tell us about British propaganda methods?

b Use Source B and your own knowledge to explain what image of Germans British propaganda showed.

c How useful is Source C as evidence of German atrocities against civilians? Use Source C and your own knowledge to answer this question.

d Is Source D a fair interpretation of how the government tried to persuade men to enlist in the First World War? Use Source D and your own knowledge to answer this question.

4 THE GREAT WAR: OUTLINE

Key Issue

- How did Germany come to be fighting on too many fronts?

1914

At first the war was what everybody had expected: a war of movement with exciting cavalry and infantry charges. The German advance through Belgium into France was stopped in September, just 60 kilometres from Paris at the Battle of the Marne. This defeat meant that Germany would have to fight on two fronts. It faced Britain and France on the Western Front and Russia on the Eastern Front.

The Germans planned to occupy the Channel ports because these would be useful as U-boat bases. But the British put a stop to the plan at the First Battle of Ypres (October–November). Ypres would be the target of two further battles in 1915 and 1917 but it stayed in British hands. The price, though, was a heavy one since German artillery shelled it into rubble and the town had to be re-built after the war.

Turkey joined the war on the side of the Central Powers (Germany and Austria–Hungary) in November. Both sides now dug trenches from the Belgian coast to the Swiss border (a distance of 700 kilometres). They settled into the kind of warfare that was to last most of the next four years: a war of trenches, barbed wire, dug-outs and machine-guns.

On the Eastern Front, the Russians mobilised their forces earlier than the Germans expected. This meant they were able to invade East Prussia – German territory. But after a heavy defeat at the Battle of Tannenberg (26–29 August), the Russian advance was halted and then pushed back.

1915

Opinions in the High Commands of both the Allied and Central Powers varied on what to do next. Winston Churchill, in command of the Royal Navy, wanted an attack on Turkey in the eastern Mediterranean to help Russia (see the Gallipoli campaign in Chapter 9). Kitchener, the commander of the army, believed the war could only be won on the Western Front and that the 'Eastern' strategy would be a waste of resources. Churchill led the group

known as the 'Easterners' and Kitchener belonged to the 'Westerners'.

At the same time, the German High Command argued over whether to concentrate on the war against Russia or on the Western Front. Generals Hindenburg and Ludendorff argued for an all-out attack against Russia. Their proposal won and General Falkenhayn was ordered to fight a defensive war in the west for the time being.

The battles of 1915 made little impact on the war. A new German weapon, gas, made a surprise and terrifying appearance in the Second Battle of Ypres (April–May). But there was no breakthrough. The British and the Australian and New Zealand Army Corps (ANZACs) tried to knock Turkey out of the war by landing at Gallipoli in Turkey. It was a complete failure. Italy joined the war on the side of the Allies (the Entente Powers Britain, France and Russia) and opened another front against the Austrians: the Italian Front.

1916

The Germans now reversed their 1915 strategy. They would win the war in the west with a massive offensive. Even if it failed, Falkenhayn told the Kaiser, France would be 'bled white' and forced out of the war. The Allies decided that their best chance of success lay in the British, French, Russians, and Italians all launching big offensives at the same time: June 1916.

1916 saw two of the biggest battles of the war: the German attack on the French at Verdun (February–December) and the mostly British attack along the River Somme (July–November). The Germans failed to capture Verdun and the British and French managed no more than a 13-kilometre advance against the Germans. The Battle of the Somme is noted for the first use by the British of their own secret weapon: the tank (see Chapters 10 and 14).

On the Eastern Front, the Russian General Brusilov had some success with his offensive against the Austrians, causing the Germans to withdraw troops from the Western Front to assist them. In fact, the most important battle of 1916 did not take place on land at all but at sea – the Battle of Jutland (see Chapter 15).

1917

The Allies continued with their 1916 strategy. Indeed, the British Prime Minister, Lloyd George, gave control of the British army in France to a French general, Nivelle. This, he hoped, would make Allied co-ordination more effective. The Germans, on the other hand, went back to their more defensive strategy of 1915. They concentrated on helping the Austrians to try to knock Italy out of the war.

1917 saw further British attempts to break through the German lines with the Third Battle of Ypres or Passchendaele (August–November). However, more important for the outcome of the war were two other events in 1917. The first event was in April when the United States entered the war on the side of the Allies. In 1918 US troops played a useful role in helping to defeat Germany.

The second event was the seizure of power by the Bolsheviks (Communists) in the Russian Revolution. They promised to pull Russia out of the war and agreed a cease-fire with Germany in December. This meant Germany could now concentrate on the Western Front at a time when American troops began to pour into Europe at the rate of 250,000 men a month.

The Western, Eastern and Italian fronts. How does the map show the difficulties Germany faced in fighting the war?

1918

Ludendorff had realised in 1917 that Germany's only hope of winning the war was on the Western Front. This victory had to come before the United States was fully involved in the war. In the meantime, the British and French generals had run out of ideas and prepared only to defend.

With Russia out of the war, Germany was able to move troops from the Eastern to the Western Front for its massive Spring or Hindenburg Offensive in March. The Allies, including the United States, halted the German advance about 80 kilometres from Paris and then launched their own counter-offensive in August. This involved 430 tanks. The exhausted German army was driven back and Germany's allies began to surrender. Bulgaria surrendered in September, Turkey in October and then Austria–Hungary on 4 November. Finally Germany itself agreed to end the war on 11 November.

British troops get some rest in their individual dug-outs.

Questions

a What was the battle in 1914 that halted the German advance into France?
b Why was this defeat a serious one for the Germans?
c How does the map show the difficulties Germany faced during the war?
d What impact did Russia's surrender have on the war?

5 THE SCHLIEFFEN PLAN

Key Issue

Why did the Schlieffen Plan fail?

If the German Schlieffen Plan had worked, the war might have been over in 1914 – and won by Germany. This chapter sets out to explain what the plan was and why it failed.

The German war plan was finalised by General Schlieffen in 1905. Schlieffen was certain that Germany would soon have to fight a war on two fronts: a war against the Russians in the east and a war against the French in the west. He knew that Germany could not win a two-front war. His plan was to knock France out of the war in just six weeks. After this, the Germans could deal with the Russians on their own.

THE PLAN IN DETAIL

Schlieffen knew that the French would be desperate to get back the two provinces of Alsace and Lorraine that they had lost to the Germans in the war of 1870–1. He deliberately kept the German forces guarding these eastern provinces weak. He hoped this would encourage the French to attack there, leaving the way clear for a surprise German attack from the north.

Schlieffen planned that the troops not used in Alsace–Lorraine would support the main attack in the north. Ninety per cent of Germany's forces in the west would invade France through Belgium and Holland. Paris would be captured and then the French would surrender. Once Germany had beaten the French, it could send its troops to the east to deal with the Russians.

The success of the Plan depended on three things. Firstly, the army in the north had to be very large and it would need troops from the southern army guarding Alsace–Lorraine. Secondly, the soldiers in the northern army would have to cover 35 kilometres a day. To do this, they would need excellent logistics. Logistics is the ability to keep troops in battle supplied with food, ammunition, and other needs. This required everything to go according to schedule. Thirdly, it was assumed that the Russians would take at least three months to get their army ready to fight.

Schlieffen died in 1913 and General von Moltke, the new Chief of Staff, took over his plan. But von Moltke lacked the nerve to take all the troops he needed from the army in Alsace–Lorraine. Instead of using 90 per cent of his troops in the northern army, he only used 60 per cent – about one million men. He was afraid the southern army would not be able to hold back a determined French attack on

Artillery, not the machine-gun, was the biggest cause of death during the war. This gun was the standard artillery piece of the British army.

Alsace–Lorraine unless it had more men. To make matters worse, Moltke decided to send 100,000 troops over to the Eastern Front because the Russians had mobilised their army in just six weeks and not the expected 12 weeks.

THE OUTCOME

Moltke gave the order to attack France and Belgium on 4 August. The Schlieffen Plan had begun. Even with their smaller numbers, the northern armies made rapid progress. They swept back the Belgian and French forces. The 75,000 men of the British Expeditionary Force (BEF), sent over from England to help the Belgians, briefly stopped 200,000 Germans at the Battle of Mons on August 23rd.

The arrival of the British took the Germans by surprise, as Schlieffen had not expected Britain to get involved in the war. The BEF at Mons had given the French time to prepare a new, stronger defensive position along the River Marne. It was then ordered to fall back, with the French, to the Marne. But the Germans were advancing too quickly. Their supplies could not keep up and their troops became exhausted and hungry. Then, when the Germans were just 60 kilometres from Paris, the French and British counter-attacked along the River Marne and drove the Germans back to the River Aisne.

The battle of the Marne (5–10 September) was the most important battle of the war. It saved Paris from capture and therefore wrecked the Schlieffen Plan. The defeat of the Plan meant Germany would have to fight the French and Russians at the same time. Germany could not win such a war. Schlieffen had known that and so did Moltke. Moltke told the German Kaiser (Emperor): 'Your Majesty, we have lost the war'. Kaiser William promptly sacked him.

STALEMATE

At the River Aisne both sides dug in and the pattern for the war was set. It would be a war fought from trenches. Gradually, both sides dug a series of trenches which stretched from the Belgian coast to the Swiss border – 700 kilometres. The Western Front moved only a little during the next four years. The land around it came to resemble a long, muddy brown scar across the face of France and Belgium.

A SOURCE

A modern history book describes the Battle of Mons (from *1914–18*, J Winter and B Baggett, 1996).

After taking up positions as best they could, the British were attacked by waves of German infantry advancing over open fields. German tactics were as outdated as the French, for which they paid dearly. For keeping to their timetable, German commanders were willing to pay in lives. But the British were too few in number to stop the German attack . . . and most of the small British army was in danger of being surrounded.

B SOURCE

One British soldier gave this account of his experience of the battle in August, 1914 in an interview in the 1970s (from *Forgotten Voices of the Great War*, M Arthur, 2002).

The company was put in a cornfield and were told to dig ourselves in. So we just made a bit of a hole in the ground and then took up a position. Then the party started when the Hun came along. We just lined up in the cornfield . . . and these Germans came in their hordes and were just shot down. But they still kept coming. There were enough of them to shove us out of the field eventually.

C SOURCE

A modern textbook's account of the Battle of Mons (adapted from *The Myriad Faces of War*, T Wilson, 1986).

By the end of the day's fighting at Mons, the commander of the BEF was making the painful discovery that his French allies were not – as he saw it – playing the game. Under pressure from the German attacks, the French were withdrawing. No attempt had been made to agree this plan with the BEF. Thus the British forces were in danger of finding themselves alone . . . So began the long struggle back to safety, known as the Great Retreat.

E SOURCE

Map of the Schlieffen Plan in action.

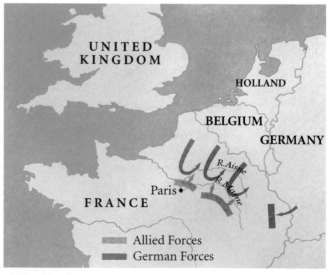

The Allied counter-attack.

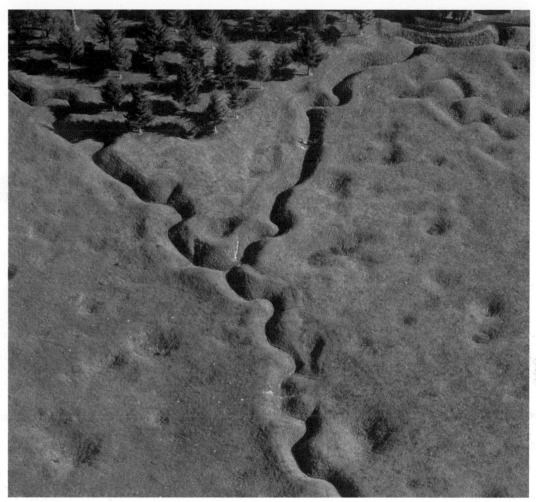

The present-day Somme still bears battle scars.

F SOURCE

A modern history book's account of the role played by the Russians in 1914 (adapted from *1914–18*, J Winter and B Baggett, 1996).

*Numerically superior, but inferior to the German Army in every other respect, the Russian Army bought time for their allies, the French. The Russians forced the Germans to strip their invading force of **divisions** pulled back to defend Germany in the east.*

Why did the Schlieffen Plan fail?
Write a few sentences under each of the following headings:
- Changes to the original plan
- Impact of the Russian mobilisation
- Failure of German logistics
- Role of the BEF

Questions

a What can you learn from Source A about the Battle of Mons?

b Does Source C support the evidence of Sources A and B about the Battle of Mons?

c How useful are Sources D and F as evidence of the reasons for the failure of the Schlieffen Plan?

d 'The Schlieffen Plan failed because of the British role at the Battle of Mons.' Use the sources, and your own knowledge, to explain whether you agree with this view.

Both sides dug trenches during the winter of 1914–15 and waited for the weather to improve before launching new attacks in the spring. But the war never became the war both sides had expected. Cavalry played no useful part and infantry attacks offered only target practice for the defenders. What followed is called a stalemate – neither side was strong enough to beat the other.

Trenches were very difficult to capture since a trench system consisted of at least three lines of trenches. The front-line trench was backed up by the support trench and behind that was the reserve trench. These trenches were connected to each other by communication trenches. Each trench was protected by rows of barbed wire up to 30 metres deep. Each section of trench would have a fire-step from which a soldier could fire or – briefly – observe the enemy trenches. Trenches were usually zig-zagged so that if the enemy captured one they would not be able to fire down its length. This shape also restricted the impact of explosions in the trenches themselves.

NO MAN'S LAND

The men also dug trenches into No Man's Land (the land in between enemy positions) to listen out for mining parties or enemy patrols at night. These trenches were called **saps**. All trenches were supposed to be deep enough to hide soldiers from enemy fire.

At regular intervals there would be a machine-gun position with each machine-gun capable of firing 450–600 rounds or bullets a minute. Such fire-power proved devastating against exposed, slow-moving infantry attacking across a No Man's Land which stretched on average for 250 metres. In some cases though, the enemy lines could be as close as 100 metres.

During enemy artillery bombardments the troops could take cover in underground bunkers. The German ones were especially deep (15 metres below ground sometimes) and well constructed because they were prepared to fight a defensive war on

enemy soil. They intended to stay where they were. The British and the French though, could not afford to fight a defensive war. They had to attack to drive the Germans out of France and Belgium.

The trenches of the Great War were supposed to look like this. Sandbags protected the soldiers at the front and the rear of the trench. In front of the sandbags was barbed wire, metres deep. A fire-step allowed the troops to raise themselves high enough to fire at the enemy when necessary.

MINING OPERATIONS

One of the purposes of saps (trenches dug out into No Man's Land) was to place listening posts in them. The men in these had sensitive listening equipment to pick up the sound of tunnels being dug beneath them. Both sides used mines in the war. These were explosives packed at the end of a long underground tunnel. The explosives were placed directly underneath the enemy's trench and then the tunnel was sealed. This sent the force of the explosion upwards. Mines could be very effective – if it was possible to dig them without being discovered.

When the mine was detonated, a huge explosion destroyed the enemy trench above it. At the same time the troops attacked while the enemy was in total confusion. At the start of the Third Battle of Ypres (or Passchendaele) in 1917, the British exploded 19 such mines under the German lines at the same time. Two were disconnected before the battle and their locations were lost. One went off in 1955 in an open field during a rain storm – the other is still out there.

If the enemy discovered the existence of a tunnel beneath them they would send out a counter-mining party. This would dig its way down to the tunnel to prevent the explosives being put in place. Ferocious fights, dozens of metres below ground, would often be the result.

The effects of a mining operation were often spectacular. But mines were not successful enough to allow an offensive to break through on a wide front.

PREPARATIONS FOR BATTLE

The High Commands of both sides were keen to break through their enemy's lines. They tried very hard to do this with a series of big attacks or offensives. Only in the last year of the war did one side achieve a decisive breakthrough.

Before big attacks or offensives took place, a number of preparations were made. Large numbers of extra troops had to be brought up to the front line. Extra ammunition and supplies were needed – not to mention coffins stacked along the roadside, in full view of the advancing troops. All of these preparations would be seen by the enemy. Aerial **reconnaissance** by aircraft meant that nothing could go on behind the lines without the enemy finding out about it. However, the biggest clue to the enemy's plans came with the heavy artillery bombardment that took place before any attack.

ARTILLERY BOMBARDMENTS

Before a big offensive both sides used their artillery to shell the enemy trenches in an effort to kill troops and destroy their trenches and barbed wire defences. Before the British Somme offensive in 1916 (see Chapter 10) the British bombardment, or barrage, lasted a week and over 1.5 million shells were fired along a 30 kilometre-wide front. The barrage was mostly ineffective and the British High Command knew this. A British intelligence report on the condition of the German trenches just before the Battle of the Somme, after the week-long British artillery bombardment, reported that 'The dug-outs are still good. The Germans appear to remain in these dug-outs all the time and are completely sheltered.' For their part, the Germans had no doubts as to what was going to happen next.

Most barrages stopped when the attackers were about to leave their trenches. This was to avoid shells dropping on your own men as they advanced across No Man's Land. However, sometimes planners used what was called a 'creeping 'or 'rolling' barrage. Here the barrage continued, just ahead of your own men, as the attack advanced. In this way, the enemy were kept in their dug-outs and couldn't fire at the attackers. The problem was that occasionally the shells dropped short and killed your own men.

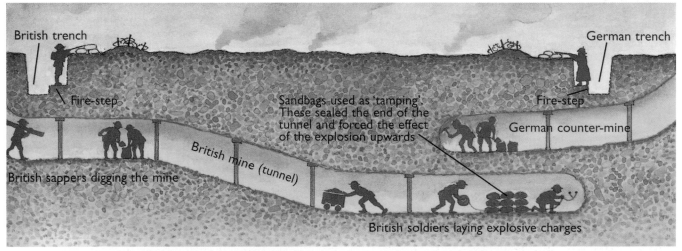

This illustration shows a mining operation. A mine has been packed into a tunnel under the German lines but a German counter-mining party is on its way. What sort of civilian job do you think gave the best preparation for this role?

'OVER THE TOP'

Before an attack could take place, paths had to be cut in your own barbed wire so your own troops could get through. This would be done at night and the paths marked with tape. This not only provided further proof of an attack but enemy machine-gunners could now direct their fire to the points where the troops would emerge.

When the order to attack was given, soldiers went 'over the top' and advanced across No Man's Land towards the enemy lines. The soldiers' task along the Somme wasn't made any easier by the order to walk towards the enemy. They didn't have to run, the High Command told them, because all the Germans would be killed in the barrage!

THE STRATEGY OF THE GENERALS

The generals were convinced that a breakthrough would come if enough troops were concentrated along a small section of the front. In this way they would outnumber the enemy, break through, and then encircle them. After that, there would only be open countryside. But this overlooked the fact that the enemy could quickly bring in reserves from another sector to plug any gaps in their front line. This was especially easy since only a small sector of the front was under attack.

It is easy to understand why so many soldiers became bitter about their generals and the strategies they used in the war.

Many historians have criticised General Haig, the commander of the British army from December 1915 until 1918, and the British commanders in general, for repeatedly using tactics which cost the lives of so many. His defenders claim that, once Haig had enough tanks and artillery, these tactics finally worked in 1918 and won the war.

A SOURCE

This photograph was taken in August 1917, during a British offensive against the Germans, called the Battle of Passchendaele. It shows British stretcher bearers carrying a wounded man.

B SOURCE

A typical trench system on the Western Front.

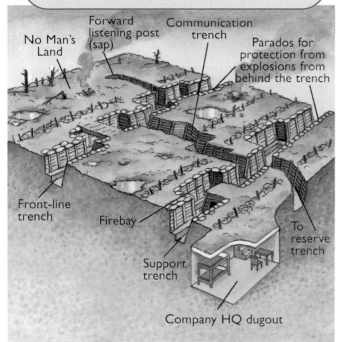

- No Man's Land
- Forward listening post (sap)
- Communication trench
- Parados for protection from explosions from behind the trench
- Front-line trench
- Firebay
- To reserve trench
- Support trench
- Company HQ dugout

C SOURCE

The view of a private in an interview for a history book (from *The First Day of the Somme*, M Middlebrook, 1971).

I cursed, and still do, the generals who caused us to suffer such torture, living in filth, eating filth, and then, death or injury, just to boost their ego.

D SOURCE

The historian, John Laffin, said this about General Haig (from *Timewatch*, BBC television documentary about General Haig).

A great commander knows exactly what he's sending his men into but Haig didn't . . . The principle which guided him was that if he could kill more Germans than the Germans could kill his men, then he would inevitably win. Now that is an appalling kind of strategy. It's not a strategy at all, it's just slaughter.

Questions

a What does Source A tell you about how the weather affected the fighting on the Western Front?

b Use Source B and your own knowledge to explain why these trenches were so difficult to capture.

c How useful is Source C as evidence of the attitude of British soldiers towards their generals? Use Source C and your own knowledge to answer this question.

d 'The generals had no real strategy at all. It was just slaughter.' Is this a fair interpretation of the role of British commanders during the war? Use Source D and your own knowledge to answer the question.

Why was it so difficult to break through the enemy's trenches?
Write a few sentences about each of the following points:
- The trench system
- Why it was difficult to launch surprise attacks
- The strategy of the generals

7 LIFE IN THE TRENCHES

Key Issue

- What was life like in the trenches?

Life in a First World War trench was mostly one of boredom and routine duties. These included replacing barbed wire, repairing and baling out flooded trenches, and digging and emptying latrines (toilets). Such duties are called 'fatigues'.

In a typical 32-day period a soldier could spend eight days in a front-line trench. Then there might be a further eight days in a reserve trench in case of an enemy attack, followed by 16 days away from the front altogether in a town or village. Every now and again though, all this would change when an offensive took place – launched either by your side or the enemy. Then the period in the trenches could last up to six weeks before relief came through. Living conditions became extremely unpleasant, as well as dangerous. However, there were occasions when the two sides could see each other as fellow men, rather than enemies.

'TRENCH FOOT'

In ideal circumstances a trench would be about two and a half metres deep with wooden duckboards along the bottom to keep feet out of the mud and water which collected there. When feet are left in water for long periods of time they can swell inside the boot, cut off circulation and rot. Frostbite could also cut off circulation. Toes were often lost in this way and sometimes even feet. This was known as 'trench foot'.

Strict measures were taken to avoid this. Men had to rub a waterproofing substance, whale oil, into their feet and soldiers would be punished if they didn't. This was necessary because some men tried to get trench foot – even at the cost of losing toes or a foot – as a way of getting a 'blighty one'. 'Blighty' was the military slang for Britain and so 'a blighty one' was a wound serious enough to get you sent home for treatment.

HYGIENE

One aspect of trench life which soldiers on both sides hated was the lack of hygiene. Latrines were pits dug in **saps** leading off the main trenches. They were about one and a half metres deep and were used as toilets. A plank of wood over the hole in the ground was the best on offer. When it was nearly full of waste it was supposed to be filled in and a new one dug. Soldiers weren't too keen on using these official facilities. This wasn't only because of their revolting smell but also because the enemy would occasionally lob shells into them on the off chance that someone might be in there.

The lack of hygiene also led to lice. These are insects which feed off the blood of their hosts. Their bites cause intense itching which leads to blisters, boils and trench fever. First World War lice – or more accurately their eggs – were almost indestructible. Body heat made them hatch out of the seams of the clothes where they were often laid.

Soldiers took comfort where they could from the war's less grim aspects. The humour of the troops helped to keep them sane. Army food was a particular target for jokes. Sausages were known as 'barkers' because of the supposedly high dog-meat content in them. Cheese was called 'bung' because of the constipation it caused.

THE CHRISTMAS TRUCE, 1914

During the Christmas of 1914 agreed cease-fires took place along two-thirds of the front between the British and the Germans. These were not official truces and were not approved by the High Commands of either side. They simply happened. There were fewer examples of such truces between the French and the Germans.

Though there were further Christmas truces in the other years of the war there were never as many as in 1914. This is because the High Commands tried hard to stop them. The generals realised that it is much harder to kill an enemy once you have exchanged food and cigarettes with him. The British High Command decided to withdraw some of the regiments involved in the 1914 truce from the front line. Sir John French, Commander-in-Chief of the British army until December 1915, was not pleased by news of the Christmas truce of 1914.

A SOURCE

Sir John French, Commander-in-Chief of the British army (quoted in *Eye Deep in Hell*, J Ellis, 1979).

[I heard of] . . . unarmed men running from the German trenches across to ours holding Christmas trees above their heads. These approaches were, in some places, well received by our men and some friendly behaviour took place. When this was reported to me, I issued immediate orders to prevent it happening again.

British and German troops meet in No Man's Land on Christmas Day in 1914.

One British soldier recalls why a truce had to be suspended (quoted in *The Price of Pity*, M Stephen, 1996).

At about lunchtime, however, a message came down the line to say that the Germans had sent across to say that their General was coming along in the afternoon, so we had better keep down, as they might have to do a little shooting to make things look right!

A soldier recalls a trench fight (from *Death's Men*, D Winter, 1979).

The Lusitania, a civilian liner, was sunk by the Germans in 1915. 1200 civilians drowned.
I saw men fighting with spades. The way the Germans yelled was awful. Some made a good fight. Some would crawl on their knees holding a picture of a woman or child in their hands above their heads but everyone was killed. The excitement was gone. We killed in cold blood because it was our duty to kill as much as we could. I thought many a time of the Lusitania. I had actually prayed for that day, and, when I got it, I killed just as much as I could.

A British soldier gives a drink to a wounded German in August 1918. Generally, the wounded were well treated by both sides and given good medical treatment.

A British sergeant of the Lancashire Fusiliers described how a Christmas truce with Germans was ended (from *Forgotten Voices of the Great War*, M Arthur, 2002).

Anyway, the generals behind must have seen it [the truce] and got a bit suspicious, so they gave orders for a battery of guns behind us to open fire and officers to fire their revolvers at the Jerries. That started the war again. We were cursing the generals to hell.

Questions

What was life like in the trenches?
Write a few sentences about each of the following points:
• Fatigues
• Rotation system
• Trench foot
• Hygiene

a What can you learn from Source A about the Christmas Truce of 1914?
b Does Source C support the evidence of Sources A and B about truces between British and German soldiers?
c Study Sources D and E. How useful are these two sources as evidence of British feelings towards Germans on the Western Front?
d 'The ordinary British soldier had no real desire to fight Germans'. Use the sources and your own knowledge to explain whether you agree with this view.

Key Issue

- What was it like to fight in a battle in the First World War?

Most soldiers did not look forward to battle but accepted it. Their sense of duty played a part in giving them the courage to 'go over the top'. But what really motivated men to face death was a sense of loyalty to their fellow soldiers: comradeship. The basic desire not to let their pals down through shirking or cowardice was very powerful.

The photograph above is of an actual dug-out recently discovered near Ypres. All the wood is the original from the war. The dug-out was originally German and was part of their defensive line in the Ypres area. It was captured by the British in 1917. Two men slept on each bunk – the four officers, though, had a bunk each. Altogether 36 men and four officers slept in the dug-out which was protected by earth and concrete. It was discovered by accident on the site of a modern brickworks and is in an excellent state of preservation. But the heavy lorries which use the site are gradually destroying the dug-out's foundations.

'COPPING A BLIGHTY'

If there was an honourable way out of the fighting, then soldiers would gladly take it. Being lightly wounded in the course of duty – 'copping a blighty' – was recognised by everyone as a decent way out of the fighting. However, self-inflicted wounds, such as shooting yourself in the foot, were seen as a coward's way out. 18-year-old Lance-Corporal Hiscock accidentally shot himself in the arm while cleaning some mud from his rifle. He was terrified of what might happen to him since such wounds usually meant a court-martial – an army trial. Hiscock's commanding officer was furious (see Source A page 22). Hiscock was lucky. His story was believed by the court but he was fined ten days' pay.

WAITING TO ATTACK

Before an attack soldiers were anxious and afraid. Attacks across open ground against an enemy with strong defences stood little chance of success and the men knew this. Once the attack started, though, many troops have said that their training took over and there was less fear. The waiting, it seems, was the worst part.

One soldier remembers waiting the night before an attack (quoted in *Death's Men* by D Winter, 1979).

All through that night I never slept a wink of sleep . . . I would find myself calculating the chances of survival. Surely a quarter of us would remain unhurt? And the other chances – what are they? Maybe one in three against being killed. One chance in four of being wounded . . . and one chance in four of being taken prisoner – as good as escaping scotfree.

The illustration on the next page shows how difficult it was to launch an attack against a well-defended enemy position and why soldiers feared 'going over the top' so much.

THE TERROR OF BATTLE

Artillery shells were the weapon soldiers feared the most. They were the biggest cause of casualties. The effect of an exploding shell on a human body was terrible. Artillery shells were designed to explode four or five metres above the ground. Jagged fragments of the red-hot iron shell and the hundreds of shrapnel balls inside them could easily tear off a limb and shatter bones.

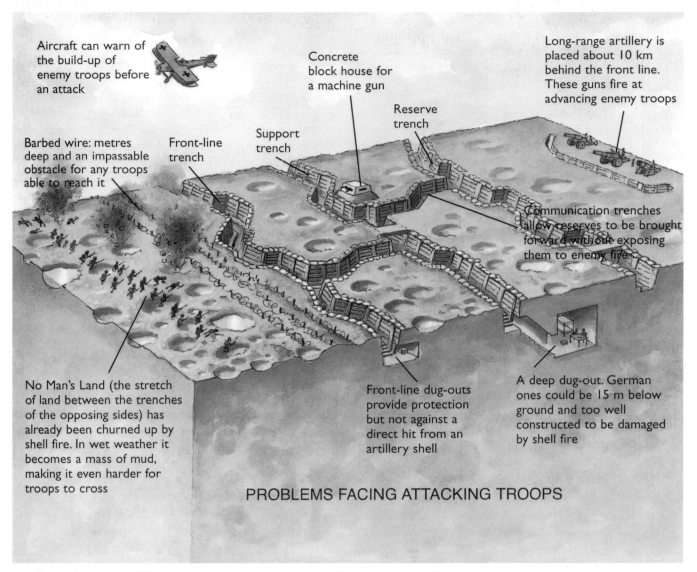

Aircraft can warn of the build-up of enemy troops before an attack

Concrete block house for a machine gun

Reserve trench

Long-range artillery is placed about 10 km behind the front line. These guns fire at advancing enemy troops

Barbed wire: metres deep and an impassable obstacle for any troops able to reach it

Front-line trench

Support trench

Communication trenches allow reserves to be brought forward without exposing them to enemy fire

No Man's Land (the stretch of land between the trenches of the opposing sides) has already been churned up by shell fire. In wet weather it becomes a mass of mud, making it even harder for troops to cross

Front-line dug-outs provide protection but not against a direct hit from an artillery shell

A deep dug-out. German ones could be 15 m below ground and too well constructed to be damaged by shell fire

PROBLEMS FACING ATTACKING TROOPS

This illustration shows how difficult it was to launch an attack against a well-defended enemy position and why soldiers feared 'going over the top' so much.

When the shell exploded, hundreds of iron balls and jagged fragments of the shell casing were driven down on the attacking troops

A typical shrapnel shell
a   Bursting charge
b   Bullets
c   Flash tube from fuze
d   Fuze

An artillery shell exploding.

High explosive shells could leave no trace of a body at all. This is one reason why the Menin Gate Memorial at Ypres lists the names of 55,000 British and Empire dead who have no grave. The names of a further 73,000 British and Empire soldiers are recorded on the memorial at Thiepval on the Somme. Their bodies were never found – blown to pieces, buried in shell holes and drowned in mud.

It was not unusual for bodies, hastily buried, to be blown up again. Men were buried very close to the lines. If they were lucky, they were later moved to more formal cemeteries in the area. Quite often, though, the record of the burial place – even the grave itself – could be lost. These men, too, would be recorded as among the missing.

Burial parties were quickly organised after a battle. Corpses could become a cause of disease if they were not buried soon afterwards.

Here is one man's experience of burying the dead (from *Death's Men* by D Winter, 1979).

As you lifted a body by its arms and legs, they detached themselves from the torso, and this was not the worst thing ... The bodies crawled with maggots ... We stopped every now and then to vomit ... the bodies had the consistency of Camembert cheese. I once fell and put my hand through the belly of a man. It was months before I got the smell out of my hands.

AN EXPERIENCE OF PASSCHENDAELE

In 1917, heavy rain turned the Third Battle of Ypres (or Passchendaele) into a pointless struggle against nature rather than the Germans. Here was a new hazard for the troops: death by drowning in mud-filled shell craters.

Captain E C Vaughan recalls his experience of Passchendaele in *Fields of Death* by P Slowe and R Woods (1986).

I paused a moment in the shell-hole; in a few seconds I felt myself sinking, and struggle as I might I was sucked down until I was firmly gripped round the waist and still being dragged in. The leg of a corpse was sticking out of the side, and frantically I grabbed it. It wrenched off and casting it down I pulled in a couple of rifles and yelled for the troops in the gun pit to throw me more.

Vaughan dragged himself out of the shell crater and gathered the few remaining men of his company together. 75 of the 90 men who had begun the attack were either dead or wounded.

THE WOUNDED

Wounded men – if they were lucky enough to be found before they died – were brought back to the **regimental aid post** for emergency treatment by stretcher bearers. From there they went to the Advanced Dressing Station. The journey to the Casualty Clearing Station was by ambulance. Here doctors carried out surgery. About half the men who died of their injuries died from head wounds. Stomach wounds were even more deadly with two out of three men dying.

Infection of the wound was a major reason for death from injury. Dirt and fragments of uniform were driven into the flesh by the bullet or piece of shrapnel and often gangrene was the result. Gangrene caused the flesh to rot and amputation – where possible – was one solution. Despite this, 'only' eight per cent of wounded men who received medical treatment died. This was largely due to the courage of the men of the Royal Army Medical Corps. Only three British soldiers have ever won the Victoria Cross twice. Two of these were medical officers.

A SOURCE

Lance Corporal Hiscock's account of his arrest for a self-inflicted wound (from *The Bloody Game*, edited by P Fussell, 1991).

'Consider yourself under arrest, Lance-Corporal Hiscock. Self-inflicted wound. They'll court-martial you for this. And you'll be lucky if they don't shoot you.' Lieutenant Clarke was, of course, nearly right. I had inflicted a wound on myself, but I knew ... that it had been done accidentally. The charge-sheet description of my 'crime', 'Self-inflicted Wound', was one of the most shameful charges possible.

B SOURCE

One survivor's memory of what motivated him to carry on fighting (from *The Price of Pity*, M Stephen, 1996).

Some people say that you come to accept death, but I don't think any of us really did. It affects you terribly when a man dies, but we had some happy times because there was such a sense of comradeship, which is impossible to understand unless you have been part of it. We would all have done anything and everything to help another man.

C SOURCE

An official photograph taken in June 1916 of British troops on their way to the Battle of the Somme.

D SOURCE

A poster issued during the war, advertising a brand of cigarettes.

TIME FOR ONE MORE

MITCHELL'S "GOLDEN DAWN" CIGARETTES.

Questions

a What does Source A tell you about the army's attitude to men who shot themselves to get out of the fighting?

b Use Source B and your own knowledge to explain why men continued to fight, despite the horror and dangers.

c How useful is Source C as evidence of the attitude of British soldiers to the war? Use Source C and your own knowledge to answer the question.

d Is Source D a fair interpretation of how soldiers went into battle? Use Source D and your own knowledge to answer the question.

9 GALLIPOLI

Key Issue

- Why was the Gallipoli campaign a failure?

In 1915 commanders on both sides realised that any battles on the Western Front would be very bloody affairs with little prospect of success. Instead, they came up with the 'weak point strategy'. Both sides tried very hard to get those countries not yet in the war on their side. Germany persuaded Bulgaria to join it and attack Serbia. Italy joined the Allies and attacked Austria–Hungary. Each side hoped that these new fronts would provide the much needed chance to break through the enemy lines. The British thought Turkey was the weak link in the Central Powers alliance of Germany, Austria–Hungary, and Turkey. A breakthrough here could unlock the stalemate on the Western Front.

ANZAC LANDINGS

Winston Churchill was in charge of the British navy in 1915. He wanted to attack Turkey through the Dardanelles Straits, seize Constantinople (the capital of Turkey), knock Turkey out of the war, and so be able to take badly needed supplies to Russia across the Black Sea. It was an ambitious plan but it went wrong from the start.

The Turks had a month's warning of the plan to land troops on the Gallipoli peninsula when an Allied naval attack in March failed disastrously as three battleships were sunk by mines. So when the British and ANZAC (Australian, and New Zealand Army Corps) forces landed on the beaches at Anzac Cove and Cape Helles in April 1915 the Turks were ready for them. They were trapped on the beaches as the Turks fired down on them from the surrounding high ground. 150,000 Allied troops were killed or wounded in the next nine months before the Gallipoli (or Dardanelles) offensive was abandoned. The only real success of the campaign was the skilful evacuation in December of the troops without a single casualty.

Churchill resigned as First Lord of the Admiralty. Instead, he served as an officer in the trenches of the Western Front. Gallipoli had proved to be anything but a 'weak point'.

FAILURE OF THE WEAK POINT STRATEGY

In general, there were no breakthroughs at Gallipoli, the Balkans or the Middle East because these fronts were considered to be side-shows. Neither side would commit enough men and resources to stage a major offensive in these places. Gallipoli also failed because the Turks got warning of the attack and because the Allied commanders under-estimated the toughness of the Turkish troops.

The failure of the Gallipoli campaign was important because it confirmed the traditional thinking of the High Commands of both sides. Each was now convinced that the war would be won or lost on the Western Front. This led to the big battles of 1916: Verdun and the Somme. Unfortunately for the men in the trenches, they went back to the same unsuccessful tactics of 1915 – attacks by massed infantry against well defended positions.

A SOURCE

From *Dictionary of Modern History*, Duncan Townson, 1998.

On 25 April, 78,000 Anzac and British troops landed on the Gallipoli peninsula but too far apart to support each other: the Anzacs were a mile north of their intended position and were faced with steep cliffs. Blunders and indecision by commanders led to both Anzac and British troops being pinned down. Another landing in August at Suvla Bay met no opposition but the lack of ability of the British commander gave the Turks time to bring up reinforcements and another stalemate followed.

B SOURCE

In August 1915, a British officer, Major Farmar, wrote this account of the fighting at Gallipoli (adapted from *The First World War*, M Brown, 2002).

In every case, attacks were ordered rather light-heartedly and carried out without method. The men on the spot were not listened to when they pointed out steps to be taken before an attack. The Turks had positioned their trenches very cleverly. Almost always in Gallipoli the attacks were made by men in the trenches and not by fresh troops.

C SOURCE

Private S T Sherwood gave this account of the landing in August 1915 at Suvla Bay on the Gallipoli peninsula, in an interview in the 1970s (from *Forgotten Voices of the Great War*, M Arthur, 2002).

We landed on Suvla beach and all that first day we were lying there with no orders to attack. Throughout the day the Turks were reinforcing their positions. By the time we had reached Point 100, which was our objective, our casualties had mounted terrifically. The Colonel turned to me and said, 'You must go down and find the Brigadier . . .' It was a verbal message. The message was 'Have reached Point 100. Casualties very heavy.'

I shot off downhill with this message. I explained the position to the Brigadier-General and he looked at me as much as to say, 'We haven't been in action two or three hours yet, it was impossible.' But a few minutes later a Lincolnshire Regiment runner came and he had the same message, their casualties were about seventy-five percent. I remember the General looking at the Major and said, 'My God, this must be true'.

D SOURCE

The Landing at Anzac Cove, on the Gallipoli peninsula, painted by George Washington Lambert.

F SOURCE

An Australian soldier, Private Henry Barnes, gave this account of the Turkish soldiers in an interview in the 1970s (from *Forgotten Voices of the Great War*, M Arthur, 2002).

The Turk was very highly regarded by me and all the men on our side. He was always a clean fighter and one of the most courageous men in the world. They faced up to the heaviest rifle fire, and nothing would stop them.

E SOURCE

The Gallipoli campaign, 1915.

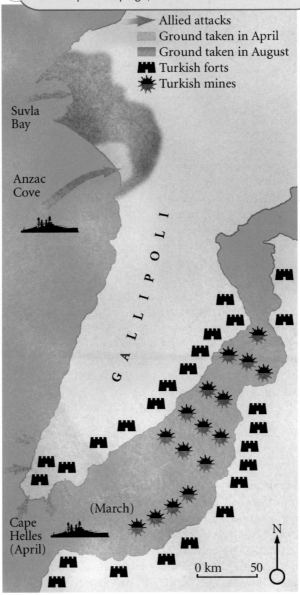

Questions

a What can you learn from Source A about the Gallipoli campaign?

b Does Source C support the evidence of Sources A and B about the way the campaign was carried out by the Allied commanders?

c How useful are Sources D and E as evidence about the Gallipoli campaign?

d 'The Gallipoli campaign failed because of bad planning.' Use the sources and your own knowledge to explain whether you agree with this view.

A German commander paid tribute to the British troops involved in the Battle of the Somme. He described them as 'lions led by donkeys'. The donkeys were the British generals who planned the offensive. The courage of the British troops was obvious, but was it a fair comment on the generals and especially General Haig – the Commander-in-Chief of the British Army?

The Battle of the Somme was planned by the British and the French together. The French role had to be cut back by about 50%, though, because they were involved in fighting off a fierce German attack at Verdun. Nonetheless, General Haig decided to go ahead with the attack. At the very least, the attack would force the Germans to move troops from their attack on the French at Verdun.

GERMANY'S 'MUDDY GRAVE'

The first day of the Battle of the Somme, 1 July 1916, was a disaster and it was soon obvious that the offensive would never succeed. 40,000 British troops were wounded and 20,000 killed. Half the troops who attacked on that day became casualties. Most of these casualties happened in the first hour of the attack. Despite this, the offensive went on until November – at the cost of 420,000 British killed and wounded. The French lost 195,000.

Recent historians have taken a more sympathetic view of General Haig and the battle itself. The poor quality of the shells fired by the British artillery during the seven-day barrage – one shell in three failed to explode – was not Haig's fault. The Germans were forced to send troops from Verdun and so pressure on the French was eased.

The German army also suffered heavily, losing many of its best junior officers (captains and lieutenants) among its 650,000 casualties. They could not be replaced. A captain in the German General Staff – the officers who planned the war – commented that: 'The Somme was the muddy grave of the German field army and of its faith in the ability of the German leaders.'

Haig has also been criticised for wasting Britain's secret weapon – the tank – by using them in such small numbers (see Chapter 14). He should have waited until there were far more available to make a really dramatic impact. But would this have made that much difference? Nearly 500 were used a year later at Cambrai but the attack still failed because the troops couldn't keep up with them. The ground gained was then quickly recaptured by the Germans.

WERE THERE ALTERNATIVES?

The military historian, John Laffin, is one of General Haig's harshest critics. He suggests that Haig should have fought the war more defensively and made the Germans do more of the attacking. In this way Britain would not have lost so many men. Laffin also criticises Haig for his failure to realise the importance of the machine-gun. Haig believed that two machine-guns per battalion (roughly 800 men) was enough. It was Lloyd George, Minister of munitions at the time, who insisted on increasing it to 16 per battalion.

Another historian, Paul Fussell, has written that even very simple (and effective) ideas for the Somme attack were ignored. One of these was to stop the British barrage for two minutes before dawn which was when most attacks took place. The Germans, thinking that an attack was about to start, would then begin flocking back to their trenches to set up their machine-guns. Another heavy barrage would then have caught the Germans out in the open.

TO RUSH OR NOT TO RUSH?

The order for the men to attack at walking pace has also been heavily criticised. The French had already developed a technique of rushing in small groups across No Man's Land, dodging in and out of shell holes for cover. This technique, known as 'rushing', limited casualties but needed troops well-trained in these tactics. The British troops who fought on the Somme, Haig believed, were not trained well enough because they were new recruits.

The French did use 'rushing' tactics during the battle – they had a bigger, trained army – and captured the German trenches opposite them in the first hour of the attack.

However, the French success could also be explained by the fact that they had twice as many heavy artillery guns in their sector of the front than the British. The French barrage was successful in

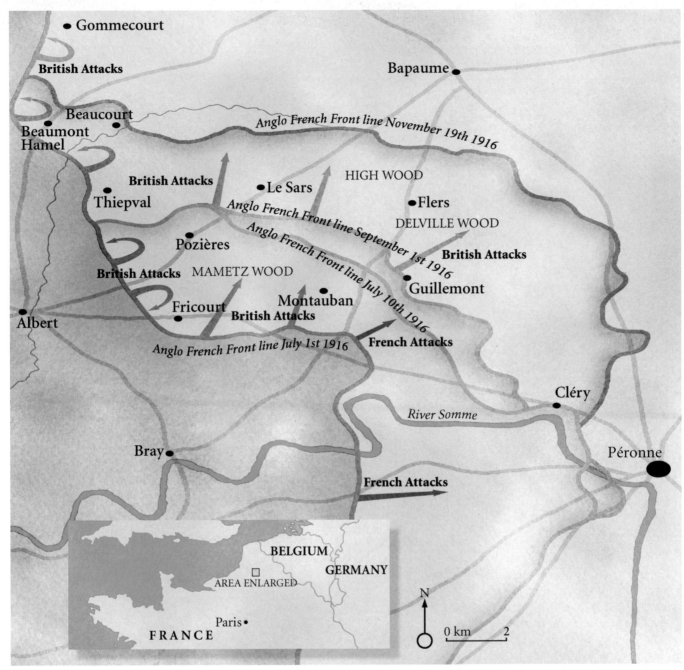

This map shows that there were some advances before the attacks ground to halt in November. The question is whether the 13-kilometre advance was worth the 620,000 British and French killed and wounded?

destroying the German dug-outs. The British barrage, with too few guns, was not. This was the key. Haig, and the man in charge of carrying out the attack, General Rawlinson, believed that the 1.5 million shells fired during the barrage would destroy the German positions. Therefore, 'rushing' tactics would not be needed. There wouldn't be any opposition!

The map above shows that there were some advances before the attacks ground to a halt in November. The question is whether the 13-kilometre advance was worth the 620,000 British and French killed and wounded? What evidence is there in the map that the French attacks did best on the first day of the battle?

A SOURCE

From a history book, *The First Day of the Somme*, M Middlebrook, 1971.

After three or four days of continuous shelling, most of the targets should have been destroyed. Of these targets the wire, a vital one for the infantry, was the only one where the damage could be easily assessed . . . The reports were inconsistent: in some places the wire was well cut; in others there were a few gaps; but in several places the wire was still intact . . . The Germans spotted some of the gaps in the British wire and their machine-guns turned these narrow alleys into death-traps.

B SOURCE

A deep, well-constructed German dug-out, captured by the British during the Battle of the Somme.

C SOURCE

From a history book, *The War Walk*, Nigel Jones, 1983.

But all this immense shellfire had not fatally damaged the enemy as the Allied Commanders had fondly hoped; far from it . . . Their defences consisted of a vast network of dug-outs, trenches, dormitories dug to depths of forty feet [12 metres] . . . This fundamental failure by the British Command to realise the strength of the enemy defences, coupled with the imperfectly cut German wire and the rigid parade-ground manner in which the infantry attacked were the main reasons for the horrible failure of the attack.

Photograph of the explosion of the British mine under the German front-line on the Hawthorn Ridge on 1 July 1916. The explosion was due to take place at 7.30 a.m., just as the British were attacking the ridge. Instead, it took place ten minutes early, tipping off the Germans that a British attack was about to begin.

F **SOURCE**

From a history textbook, *Eye Deep in Hell*, J Ellis, 1976.

The British often made the German's task easier. To allow their own troops to get into No Mans Land it was necessary to cut gaps in the British wire just before the attack. As one soldier who was there remarked: 'The advertisement on our front was absurd. Paths were cut and marked days before. Small wonder the German machine-gun fire was directed with such fatal precision'.

E **SOURCE**

Lieutenant B L Gordon of the King's Own Yorkshire Light Infantry's account, written three days after the attack of 1 July (quoted in *The Somme*, Malcolm Brown, 1996).

Although our bombardment had failed to knock out the enemy machine-guns, its effect upon the trenches had been very great. For the most part, they were entirely knocked in. In places one came to a trench in good condition but this was rare. The German machine-guns and infantry must have been preserved owing to their deep dugouts, most of them 30 or 40 feet [9–12 metres] below ground level. The enemy barbed wire positions had every-where been completely destroyed by our artillery.

Questions

a What can you learn from Source A about the British artillery barrage at the start of the Battle of the Somme?

b Does Source C support the evidence of Sources A and B about the British attack?

c How useful are Sources D and E as evidence of the effectiveness of the British attack?

d 'The British offensive on the Somme was a failure because the attack was badly planned.' Using the sources and your own knowledge, explain whether you agree with this view.

11 THE EASTERN FRONT

Key Issue

- Why was Russia defeated?

After some early success against the Germans in August 1914, the Russians were forced back after the Battle of Tannenberg. A second major defeat for the Russians at the Masurian Lakes in September meant that they would have to fight the war on Russian, rather than German, soil. The German commanders, Generals Hindenburg and Ludendorff, became national heroes.

Nonetheless, despite these defeats, the Russian contribution to the war was already vital. The Germans were forced to withdraw troops from the Western Front to deal with the Russians. This helped the French to defeat the German Schlieffen Plan.

RUSSIAN SUCCESS

The Russians did better against the Austrians but the Germans quickly came to the aid of their allies. In 1915, Tsar Nicholas, who had no real military abilities, foolishly decided to take command of the Russia army. By the end of 1915 the Russian army had retreated 500 kilometres with one million men killed. But the Russians were far from finished. In June 1916 General Brusilov launched a massive, surprise offensive against the Austrians and made some striking advances. Within a week the Russians advanced 60 kilometres and took 70,000 prisoners. Brusilov, though, found it difficult to keep his troops supplied and the Germans and Austrians withdrew troops from other fronts to prop up the Austrian Eastern Front army. The attacks came to a halt in October.

Despite the eventual failure of the campaign, the Russians had again come to the aid of their allies. The British and French were relieved to see German troops withdrawn during the Battles of the Somme and Verdun. The Italians were helped for the same reason. The Austrians lost 740,000 men killed, wounded or taken prisoner and it was at this point that the armies of the Austro–Hungarian Empire lost their will to fight. Austria only fought on because the Germans sent troops to help it. However, the Russians could scarcely afford their one million casualties either. The Emperor of Russia, Tsar Nicholas II, was to pay the price for this military failure in 1917 with the loss of his throne and then his life and the lives of his family.

REVOLUTION

There was a real breakthrough on the Eastern Front in 1917 but it was a German one: Russia's withdrawal from the war. The Tsar was overthrown in March 1917 by a people fed up with the loss of life, and the hardships which the war caused. However, the new government led by Kerensky made the mistake of carrying on with the unpopular war. In November 1917 Lenin and his Bolshevik or Communist Party forced Kerensky from power in a revolution. They agreed a cease-fire with Germany within five weeks. The Germans were now able to move huge numbers of troops over to the Western Front for their final offensive of the war in March 1918.

WHY WAS RUSSIA DEFEATED?

Russia lost the war for a mixture of military, economic and political reasons. The Russian army was not sufficiently well organised or led to fight a war on a front which was 1800 kms long – more than twice the length of the Western Front. Perhaps more serious was the way the people turned against the Tsar. The civilians suffered shortages of food and fuel and blamed him. Equally seriously, so did the ordinary soldiers and even their commanders.

Nonetheless, Russia's role in the war was a vital one, despite its surrender to Germany in March 1918. The Germans had to fight a war on two fronts because of Russia's involvement and this made the threat facing the British and French from the Germans much less serious. Russian attacks in August 1914 and again in 1916 came at crucial moments and forced Germany to weaken its own forces.

A SOURCE

A British nurse describes her experiences on the Russian front (from *Nurse at the Russian Front*, F Farmborough, 1974).

A young artillery officer came to seek advice from our medical staff. He was depressed by the recent defeat and criticised the High Command. 'They do not realise how exhausted our men are,' he cried. 'In their comfortable armchairs in their hotels far from the fighting, with the war-maps stretched before them, they put their finger on a town – "Ah", they say, "this must be seized by our men within the next three days!" And the command goes out! And our men, hungry, cold and tired to death, are expected to spring into action . . . and sweep everything before them – no matter what the cost.'

B SOURCE

These German and Russian soldiers are reacting to the news of Russia's withdrawal from the war in December 1917. The ones with the fur hats are Russians.

Waffenruhe an der Ostfront.
Beim Tauschhandel.

C SOURCE

A Russian soldier, Mikhail Rosenthal, describing army morale in 1917 (quoted in a modern history book, *The People's Century*, G Hodgson, 1995).

*I didn't feel like fighting any more, there was no one to fight for when Nicholas gave up the throne. It was chaos. The people supposed to give us logistical support [supplies] ran away first. We began to go hungry. We were all very dirty . . . At the end of the war there were few people left who could give orders. Our **division** didn't exist. We were very happy that we were free to run away.*

D SOURCE

A Russian general, Alekseev, wrote this report in April 1917 to the Minister of War, after the Tsar had been overthrown (adapted from *Octobrists to Bolsheviks*, M McCauley, 1984).

The situation grows worse every day. Information coming in from all sides indicates that the army is falling apart.

1. *Desertions continue all the time . . .*
2. *Discipline declines with each passing day . . .*
3. *The authority of officers and commanders has collapsed and cannot be restored . . . the morale of the officers has sunk to a new low.*
4. *A mood for peace has developed in the ranks.*
5. *Anti-war **propaganda** is circulating in the army.*

E SOURCE

This Russian poster from 1915 appeals to Russians' sense of history as well as their patriotism. It shows a Russian knight from medieval times slaying the Central Powers' dragon. He has already cut off its Austrian head, cut through the neck of the German and is about to slice off the Turkish head. In the background are the ruins of towns destroyed by the Germans in Europe.

Questions

a What can you learn from Source A about the morale of the Russian army during the war?

b Does Source C support the evidence of Sources A and B about the morale of the Russian army during the war?

c How useful are Sources D and E as evidence of Russian attitudes to the war?

d 'The Russian army collapsed because of poor leadership'. Using the sources and your own knowledge, explain whether you agree with this view.

Key Issue

- What was the impact of gas on the war?

The Great War favoured the defenders. Any new weapons mostly helped those who defended trenches rather than those who attacked them. The machine-gun was the supreme defensive weapon.

A brand new weapon like gas made no real impact on the war. It was first used by the Germans in April 1915. It was a total surprise to the Allies and a nasty one at that. But soon they were able to use counter-measures against its effects – though the first of these counter-measures, a cloth soaked in urine held over the face, lacked a certain appeal. The defenders could also light fires along their trenches. The hot air lifted the gas clouds above the men and out of danger. But such methods were not really practical.

TYPES OF GAS

The first type of gas used was chlorine. It immediately caused choking and then stripped away the lining of the lungs. Victims died from suffocation. But chlorine had two serious disadvantages: it could be seen and its effect was immediate. By the end of 1915 the Germans had found a more deadly type of gas: phosgene. This was 18 times more deadly than chlorine and could not be seen. Even worse, men who breathed it suffered only minor discomfort at first and therefore breathed in larger doses. Sometimes it was only 24 hours later that the terrible effects took place. The spasms of vomiting could then last for 48 hours. The lungs filled up with yellow liquid and the victims died from drowning.

Gas masks, first introduced in 1916, were effective against both these gases. But no counter-measure was ever found against another German gas, first used in 1917: mustard gas. Unlike the others, mustard gas was not that deadly. Only 2% of its victims died. It attacked the surface of the skin and caused intense burning, swelling of the eyes, blindness and choking. Heavy doses could cause the exposed flesh to be eaten away. From July 1917 to the end of the war, mustard gas caused 14% of all battle casualties.

Nevertheless, the development of the gas mask meant that after 1916 only 3% of gassed soldiers actually died and 93% were able to return to duty. Changes in wind direction also made it a dangerous and unpredictable weapon since the wind could easily blow the gas back against its users.

A SOURCE

Sergeant Jack Dorgan gave this account of the first use of gas in April 1915 in an interview in the 1970s (from *Forgotten Voices of the Great War*, M Arthur, 2002).

But we'd only gone a hundred yards in front of the Canadians when we encountered the gas. We'd had no training for gas prevention, never heard of the gas business. Our eyes were streaming with water and pain, and all we had was a roll of bandages ... So we bandaged each other's eyes, and anyone who could see would lead a line of half a dozen or so men, each with his hand on the shoulder of the one in front.

B SOURCE

Henry Tonks was with the artist, John Sargent, who painted Source D. Tonks described this scene at Le Bac-du-Sud in July 1918, in a letter in 1920 (adapted from an extract in *The First World War*, M Brown, 2002).

Gassed cases kept coming in, led along in parties of about six, just as Sargent had painted them. They sat or lay down on the grass, there must have been several hundred, evidently suffering a great deal, chiefly from their eyes which were covered up by lint bandages. The gas was mustard gas which causes temporary blindness from swelling of the eyes. Sargent was very moved by the scene and immediately began making a lot of notes.

C SOURCE

Official statistics for casualties and deaths caused by gas in the British army, 1915–18.

Year	Casualties	Deaths
1915	12,792	307
1916	6698	1123
1917	52,452	1796
1918	113,764	2673

SOURCE

A painting, *Gassed*, by the war artist, John Sargent, of a scene he witnessed at Le Bac-du-Sud in France, in July 1918.

SOURCE

E Photograph of British gas casualties in April 1918.

SOURCE

F This is an account of the use of gas by the British against the Germans at the Battle of Loos in September, 1915 (adapted from *The Myriad Faces of War*, T Wilson, 1986).

There was nothing more than the drift of some cigarette smoke and a rustling of leaves in some poplar trees to suggest a favourable wind. Yet on this basis, the go-ahead was given. As a result, the gas achieved far less than it might have done. At some points it did reach the German front line and took the Germans by surprise. At others, the gas came to a stop in No Man's Land or moved across so slowly that the attacking troops got in front of it. At other places, it blew back into the British trenches.

Questions

a What can you learn from Source A about the first use of gas in April 1915?

b Does Source D support the evidence of Sources A and B about the effects of gas?

c How useful are Sources C and E as evidence about the impact of gas?

d 'Gas was a terrifying but, in the end, unsuccessful weapon.' Using the sources and your own knowledge, explain whether you agree with this view.

When the war broke out in 1914 few people expected that aircraft would play an important role. The French commander, Marshall Foch, described them as 'useless'. Yet by the end of the war, the French had built 68,000 planes and 52,000 of these were lost in battle.

RECONNAISSANCE

Nonetheless, it is easy to see why so few had any faith in aircraft as a weapon of war. The top speed of a typical British fighter plane in 1914 was just 72mph. Army commanders thought the only useful role for aircraft would be **reconnaissance** or spying missions over enemy territory. Planes could easily discover enemy troop movements and this could indicate if an offensive was being planned. Aerial photographs were studied for any signs of disturbed earth. Perhaps a tunnel was being dug or new gun pits for artillery were being prepared. This was probably the most valuable role for aircraft but it wasn't the only one.

'SPOTTING'

They also provided a useful service as 'spotters'. Spotters told the artillery how accurate their fire was and what changes were needed to get the shells to hit their targets. This was necessary because often the artillerymen couldn't see where their shells were falling since they could be five kilometres or more away. However, it was a slow process because pilots could only communicate with the artillery by dropping messages to them. It could take two hours to spot for just four guns.

NEW TECHNOLOGY

British aircrew got a nasty surprise in October 1915. Both sides were used to being shot at by anti-aircraft guns from the ground and by other planes in the air.

But in October the German had a fighter plane, the Fokker, which could fire a machine gun through the propeller without shooting it to bits. When these pilots aimed their aircraft at enemy, they were also aiming their gun. So successful was this plane that the Royal Flying Corps (RFC), later changed to the Royal Air Force (RAF), could only send out reconnaissance planes if they were escorted by three fighters as protection. This limited the effectiveness of the reconnaissance information available to the British army. It was not until mid-1916 that the RFC had a plane which had the same capability as the German fighter.

GROUND ATTACK

From 1916 onwards aircraft became more and more involved in ground attack operations. Planes now carried a bigger bomb load and this made them more useful in bombing and machine-gunning enemy trenches. The British Handley Page bomber, in service from 1917, could carry 16 50kg bombs or one large 750kg bomb. This aircraft, and others like it, proved effective against ships and they were used at night to bomb factories, railway junctions and docks in Germany.

On 8 August 1918, during the Allied counter-offensive against the Germans, nearly 2000 British and French aircraft supported the attack. The Allies decided to bomb the bridges over the River Somme to stop the Germans retreating across the river. The bridges were attacked for two days but not one was destroyed and the RAF lost nearly 150 planes.

CASUALTIES

During the course of the war, over 50,000 aircrew on all sides were killed. Some of the lives of the RFC pilots could have been saved if they had been allowed to use parachutes. The army commanders decided, however, that if pilots had parachutes they might jump out when attacked, instead of staying with their planes. Policies like this help to explain why the average life expectancy of a pilot on the Western Front was about two weeks.

A French 'spad' shoots down a German plane.

Questions

a What were the three major roles of aircraft in the war?

b Which of these three roles do you think was most important and why?

c Why do you think the ability of the Fokker to fire through its propeller was such an advantage?

d Pilots didn't live very long. Why, then, were so many men keen to volunteer to serve as pilots?

How effective were gas and aircraft as new weapons?

Write a few sentences on each of the following points:

• Different types of gas and their effects
• Weaknesses of gas as a weapon
• Main uses of aircraft
• Technological improvements in aircraft during the war
• Most effective use of aircraft was . . .

The stalemate on the Western Front was eventually broken in 1918 and a new weapon did play a part in this. The new weapon was the tank. To keep it as secret as possible the machine was described as a 'water tank'. Its official title was 'Trench Crossing Machine'. But it was the word 'tank' which stuck. Its major purpose was to break through the enemy barbed wire, clear their trenches with machine-guns and destroy their machine-gun posts. Then the infantry could follow through. Unlike other weapons, this one had a clear role as a weapon of attack.

The tank had a maximum speed – on a good road – of about six kilometres per hour. It was protected by about 10 millimetres of steel armour and could carry either four machine-guns or two cannon. Some carried large bundles of wooden stakes, called a fascine, to drop into the enemy trenches so that they could cross them. Others had large hooks which they used to drag away entanglements of barbed wire. Tanks had a crew of eight who had to face many problems. Bullets fired at tanks caused steel splinters on the inside to break away so the crew had to wear steel masks to protect their eyes and face. They broke down, got stuck in mud and moved slowly. This made them an easy target for artillery.

The commander of the new tank corps, Lieutenant-Colonel Swinton, wanted to use the tank in large numbers. This, he claimed, would bring the maximum benefit from the element of surprise. General Haig disagreed. He wanted to use them as soon as possible so that the experience gained would help train tank crews in real combat methods. At that time no one really knew what tanks could do and what tactics to use with them.

A SOURCE

This photograph shows a British tank stuck in a German second line trench, after the Battle of Cambrai in 1917.

TANKS ON THE SOMME

Haig decided that tanks would be used during the Battle of the Somme in September 1916. The battle was going badly and the tank would be a big boost for the morale of both the soldiers and the civilians.

Only 49 were used in the battle but 17 of these broke down before they even got to the British lines. Of the 32 left, 18 managed to attack the German lines and were successful enough to convince the Allied High Command that they must be used in greater numbers. Haig ordered 1000 tanks to be built.

Tanks played an important role in the final Allied offensive of August 1918 when 430 were used but the losses were very high. There were only six left after just five days but the initial breakthrough had been achieved. The Germans, from now on, would retreat until they surrendered in November.

Some historians have suggested that it was more successful as a psychological weapon because of the fear it caused among the Germans. Others believe that it was a success because of the way it broke through the enemy lines for the infantry to follow.

B SOURCE

A German war correspondent at the front wrote (quoted in *The War in the Trenches*, A Lloyd, 1976):

When the German troops crept out of their dug-outs in the mist of the morning and stretched their necks to look for the English, their blood chilled. Mysterious monsters were crawling towards them over the craters . . . Nothing stopped them . . . Someone in the trenches said, 'The devil is coming', and word was passed along the line. Tongues of flame leapt from the sides of the iron caterpillars . . . the English infantry came in waves behind.

C SOURCE

An artist's impression of a British tank attack at the Battle of Cambrai in November 1917.

D SOURCE

Lieutenant F Mitchell's account of a tank attack on a German pillbox (concrete strongpoint) in August 1917.

The walls of the pillbox were shellproof but the door was soon blown away. Most of the garrison was killed by the tank's fire, and few of those who got out escaped the raking machine-gun fire of the sinking tank . . . There were 29 casualties [among the British troops] instead of a thousand. The tank had shown its qualities.

Questions

a What can you learn from Source B about the effectiveness of tanks as a weapon?

b Use Source A and your own knowledge to explain the limitations of tanks as a weapon.

c How useful is Source C as evidence of the way tanks were used during the war? Use Source C and your own knowledge to answer this question.

d 'The tank had shown its qualities.' Is this an accurate interpretation of the role of tanks during the war? Use Source D and your own knowledge to answer the question.

15 THE WAR AT SEA

Key Issue

- Why was the war at sea important in deciding the outcome of the war?

There was only one really big naval battle in the First World War – the Battle of Jutland in May 1916. Over 250 ships on both sides were involved and 10,000 sailors were killed or wounded. However, the war at sea was also fought under it, as well on its surface. Germany's U-boats or submarines seriously threatened Britain's **supply lines** and at one stage in 1917 Britain came close to running out of food.

THE U-BOAT CAMPAIGN AGAINST BRITAIN

Submarines were another new weapon and they sank a great deal of British **merchant ships**. Merchant ships were essential to Britain because it needed to import so much of its food and supplies. At one stage in 1917 Britain had only two months' supply of wheat and flour. Despite this success, the Germans never sank enough merchant ships to bring Britain to the point of asking for peace terms from Germany.

At first, German U-boats sank only the ships of Britain and its allies. The ships of neutral countries in British waters were not attacked. But in February 1915 the German government declared that any ship around Britain would be attacked – including the ships of countries not at war. This is called unrestricted submarine warfare. This led to a steady rise in the number of sinkings of ships.

THE SINKING OF THE LUSITANIA

Up to February 1915, the U-boats had sunk only 10 British merchant ships. In August 1915 alone they sank 42 merchant ships. This campaign, though effective in causing severe shortages in Britain, was controversial. For one thing, civilian liners were included in the list of targets. As a result many women and children were drowned. In May 1915 the British passenger liner the *Lusitania* was on its way from the United States to Britain. It was sunk by a U-boat with the loss of 1200 lives.

The sinking of the *Lusitania* by a German U-boat caused tremendous outrage in Britain and the United States. The British government knew, of course, that the ship was carrying an illegal and secret cargo of ammunition to Britain. The explosion of this ammunition helps to explain why the ship sank in fewer than 20 minutes. This really made it a fair target for a U-boat – though the U-boat commander didn't know about the secret cargo. The British government, of course, made no mention of the ammunition when it fiercely attacked the Germans for the sinking.

The sinking of the *Lusitania* was a political disaster for the Germans. It added still more evidence to the British campaign to portray the Germans as barbarians and murderers. It also enraged US opinion because, among the dead, were 128 Americans. The United States was not a country the Germans could afford to anger.

ANTI-SUBMARINE MEASURES

The British navy tried desperately to come up with ideas to beat the U-boat threat. Feelings against the German navy were running high – and not just because of the activities of the U-boats. In December 1914 German cruisers had shelled three English east coast towns, killing and wounding 700 civilians.

As a defence against U-boats, the depth charge – an explosive device set to go off at a pre-set depth under water – was effective. But they were available only in small numbers and the U-boat had to be located first. That was the hardest task of all. **Hydrophones** were being developed to detect the sound of U-boat engines under water but they were not yet sensitive enough.

Another anti-submarine measure was the Q-ship, which to begin with proved fairly successful. A Q-ship was a warship disguised as an unarmed merchant ship. U-boat commanders preferred to sink merchant ships by surfacing and using their deck gun. In this way they could save their supply of torpedoes for more dangerous targets such as cruisers or battleships.

When a U-boat surfaced for an easy 'kill' against what it thought was an unarmed merchant ship, the more powerful guns of the Q-ship would blast it out of the water. Equipping ordinary merchant ships with guns of their own also helped to discourage surface attacks. U-boat commanders, therefore, soon learned to be more cautious and had to decide whether a lone merchant ship was really worth a precious torpedo.

However, these measures were not really very effective. Only 15 U-boats were sunk in the whole of 1916. By the end of that year Germany had 140 submarines. What really saved Britain was the German worry about the attitude of the United States to German attacks on their ships. The Germans suspended their campaign of unrestricted submarine warfare around British waters in October 1915 after American protests. They resumed it in early 1916 and then called it off again in May of that year. Despite this, on average one in every four merchant ships leaving British ports was being sunk.

THE CONVOY SYSTEM

In April 1917 the Royal Navy introduced the convoy system of grouping merchant ships together and protecting them with anti-submarine warships called destroyers. This was done at the insistence of David Lloyd George, Prime Minister since December 1916. The convoy system proved very effective in discouraging U-boat attacks. In 1918, only one out of every 25 merchant ships was sunk.

Convoys were not effective because destroyers sank more U-boats. The main reason was because a convoy of 20 ships wasn't much easier to spot in a vast ocean than a single ship on its own. Therefore, a U-boat's chances of sighting a merchant ship were effectively only one-twentieth of what they had been. When a U-boat did find a convoy it had time to attack one or maybe two merchant ships before destroyers began depth-charging it. The rest of the convoy could then make its escape.

On 1 February 1917 the German High Command decided to gamble, once again, on re-opening its campaign of unrestricted submarine warfare. The Germans believed that Britain could be brought to its knees in six months as a result of the U-boat **blockade** of British ports. Neutral countries would stop trading with Britain to avoid having their ships sunk.

THE END OF AMERICAN NEUTRALITY

The United States had stayed out of the war in 1914 and intended to keep out. Americans saw the war in Europe as just another squabble between greedy European powers trying to expand their empires. The Kaiser was warned by his advisers that the policy of unrestricted submarine warfare would probably bring the United States into the war. They were right. The United States declared war on 6 April 1917. However, this wouldn't matter, they said, because, by the time the very small American army was big enough and trained, the war would be over. Even if it was not, the United States wouldn't have enough ships left to transport its troops across the Atlantic.

One further development which helped bring the US into the war was the Zimmerman telegram. Zimmerman was the German Foreign Minister. He foolishly sent a coded telegram to the Mexican government. In this he offered the Mexicans a large part of the southern United States if Mexico declared war on the US. The states of New Mexico, Texas and Arizona would be given to Mexico after America's defeat. The British decoded the telegram at the end of February 1917 and passed it on to an outraged President Wilson.

In the short term, though, the situation did not look good for Germany. In 1914, the American navy was the third largest in the world after Britain and Germany. Its destroyers could now be used on convoy duty to protect merchant shipping routes between Britain and the United States. Britain's food supply problems improved immediately. Wheat, for example, could now be imported from the United States instead of Australia, which was much further away. The American government was also willing to lend Britain money so it could buy its vital supplies from the United States – something the Americans had refused to do before 6 April.

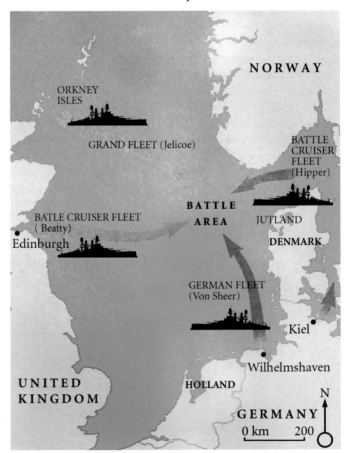

The Battle of Jutland.

However, the German advisers got it wrong – eventually. At first, Britain's shipping losses were crippling. 127 ships were sunk by U-boats in March 1917 alone and 211 in August. But Britain's use of the convoy system dramatically cut merchant ship losses and it was not forced to beg for peace. Instead, American troops poured into France in 1918 at the rate of 250,000 a month. These fresh and enthusiastic troops were important in the successful Allied offensive of August 1918 which broke Germany's will to fight on.

THE BATTLE OF JUTLAND, MAY 1916

Clearly the defeat of Germany's U-boat campaign was vital in preventing a German victory. However, the battle fought between the British and German fleets off the coast of Jutland in the North Sea also had a decisive impact on the outcome of the war.

The British Grand Fleet was commanded by Admiral Jellicoe and the German High Seas Fleet by Vice Admiral Scheer. On 31 May the two fleets opened fire at a range of 15 kilometres from each other at about half-past three in the afternoon.

The German gunners were more accurate and, it seems, their shells more destructive. Two of Admiral Beatty's battle cruisers, the *Indefatigable* and the *Queen Mary* were sunk by huge internal explosions. A devastated Beatty could only comment: 'There seems to be something wrong with our bloody ships today.' HMS *Invincible* was sunk later that day in a similar way. She sank in fifteen seconds, blown in two. With her back broken, the *Invincible* went down in a V shape (see Source C). All but six of her crew of 1031 men perished with it.

German shells had pierced the thinly armoured gun turrets of the British ships and started fires. These fires then exploded the ships' magazines – the store deep below decks where the ammunition was kept. However, the Germans lost ships too. The German commander, Scheer, decided that he could not afford to lose more ships because his fleet was smaller than that of the British. Under the cover of night, the German fleet made its escape from the battle.

WHO WON?

Jellicoe's losses were much greater than those of Scheer. The British lost 14 ships – three of them powerful battle cruisers – and 6000 men were killed. The German losses were 11 ships but only one of these was a battle cruiser. 2550 German sailors died. The Germans claimed a victory because of the heavier British losses.

This may be true but winning naval battles is about more than tactical issues like sinking enemy ships. More important are the strategic consequences which affected the outcome of the entire war. The fact is the Germans were desperate to break the blockade of their ports by the British fleet and this they failed to do. Instead, the British blockade continued without interference from the German fleet, which stayed bottled up in its base at Kiel for the rest of the war.

The German withdrawal gave the Royal Navy control of the seas and it was able to prevent vital supplies reaching German ports. Gradually the German population went hungry and as many as 750,000 German civilians died as a result of diseases caused by their poor diet. This broke the morale of the 'Home Front' and led to food riots in 1918. Morale on the German military front collapsed as a result. The British naval blockade was, therefore, a key factor in Germany's surrender in November 1918. These were the strategic consequences of Jutland.

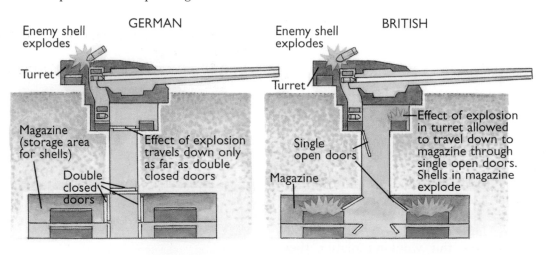

Illustration of the differences in the way British and German gun turrets were designed.

SOURCE

A British poster about the shelling by the German navy of Scarborough in 1914.

MEN OF BRITAIN !
WILL YOU STAND THIS ?

Nº 2 Wykeham Street, SCARBOROUGH, after the German bombardment on Decr 16th. It was the Home of a Working Man. Four People were killed in this House including the Wife, aged 58, and Two Children, the youngest aged 5.

78 Women & Children were killed and 228 Women & Children were wounded by the German Raiders

ENLIST NOW

B ## SOURCE

A German sailor recorded his reaction to the Battle of Jutland (from *1914–18*, J Winter and B Baggett, 1996).

On June 2 news reaches us that the largest naval action ever fought took place off Horns Reef on the Skagerrak. The action concluded with an undoubted defeat of the British fleet. Several British battleships were destroyed.

D ## SOURCE

A British history book, *The First World War*, M Brown, 2002, on the Battle of Jutland.

However, overall the victory could be said to go to the British because the German High Seas Fleet thereafter played no role in the war ... until it came out to surrender in November 1918.

C ## SOURCE

Battleships in Action at Jutland by Robert H. Smith.

Questions

a Why was Source A produced by the British government?

b Use Source B and your own knowledge to explain why this sailor believed Jutland was a German victory.

c How useful is Source C as evidence about the Battle of Jutland?

d Is Source D a fair interpretation of the Battle of Jutland? Use Source D and your own knowledge to answer the question.

'Why was the war at sea important at deciding the outcome of the war?'

Write a few sentences under the following headings:
- U-boat campaign
- Naval blockade
- Battle of Jutland
- Sinking of the Lusitania
- US entry into the war

At the beginning of 1918 no one would have believed that the war would be over within 11 months. It seemed set to go on for at least another two years. But it did end – and with a German defeat. Why? Part of the answer lies with the role of the Americans. There were 325,000 American troops in France in April and two million of them by the end of the war. But more significant was the collapse in morale of the German armed forces and German civilians.

LUDENDORFF'S SPRING OFFENSIVE

The German High Command launched its massive assault at the point where the British and French sectors joined together. They had the advantage of more men. Ludendorff, the German commander on the Western Front, had been able to bring over 52 **divisions** (about 750,000 troops) fresh from their victory over the Russians. These troops were confident and highly trained in Ludendorff's new 'infiltration tactics'.

The attack, on 21 March, was launched after a very heavy but short five-hour artillery barrage from half-past four in the morning. Ludendorff told his troops not to attack the British lines along the whole 100-kilometre front but to infiltrate in small numbers where the most damage had been done. Where the British positions were still strong, the Germans simply went round them. These 'shock' troops then made for the British artillery and eliminated it so that the rest of the German advance would not be wiped out by the British guns.

The tactics were stunningly successful. On the first day, the Germans broke through the British lines for an eight-kilometre advance – the same distance the British had fought for five months to achieve on the Somme in 1916. The Germans came within 60 kilometres of Paris in late May. But their casualties were as great as the defenders' and the troops soon became exhausted. A worrying development for the Germans was that their hungry troops stopped to loot food from farms. They had moved too fast to be protected by their own artillery. In late July the Allies struck back.

THE ALLIED COUNTER-OFFENSIVE: 8 AUGUST

The British, French, Canadian, Australian and American forces were, for the first time, under the control of a single commander, France's Marshall Foch. This made sure that the Allied troops worked together according to a common plan. The exhausted German troops, faced by fresh Americans and over 600 tanks, gave up. They hadn't had the time to strengthen their defences in the areas they had only just occupied. Germans surrendered in huge numbers. They decided that the war could not be won.

Germany's allies began to drop out of the war: Bulgaria in late September, Turkey in late October and Austria in early November. Kaiser Wilhelm gave up the throne of Germany on 9 November and Germany's new civilian government accepted an **armistice** at 11 o'clock on the morning of 11 November.

THE GERMAN HOME FRONT

The German army at the end of 1918 could have fought on, but it didn't want to. The civilian population had turned against the war. The British naval **blockade** of German ports caused severe food shortages. Many thousands of Germans died as a result of common illnesses because of their very poor diet. Strikes, caused not only by terrible shortages but also by ideas of Communist revolution, reduced factory production. The navy **mutinied** in late October rather than obey a last, desperate order to take on the British navy.

The powerful groups in Germany – the factory owners and landowners – also realised that if they continued fighting a war they could not win, then they risked something worse than a lost war. They risked losing all their wealth in a Communist revolution like the one in Russia in 1917. Hindenburg and Ludendorff shared these worries and they told the Kaiser that the war must end before it was too late.

Germany had launched 'Operation Michael' in March 1918 in the desperate hope that Germany might win the war before the United States could become fully involved. What the Germans had failed to realise was that the United States was already making a real contribution to the Allied cause. It was measured in steel and iron – not troops.

A SOURCE

Herbert Sulzbach was a German officer. Here he describes a visit on leave to his home town, Frankfurt, in October 1918 (quoted in *Forgotten Voices of the Great War*, Max Arthur (editor), 2002).

I went through the streets of Frankfurt. I was not saluted [by ordinary soldiers]. Everything was rationed and there was hardly anything to buy . . . and the mood of the people was really bad. We hadn't realised at the Front how bad it was at home. People were really fed up with war. They wanted the war to be ended as soon as possible, victory or no victory . . . Some of my comrades received letters which were most upsetting. Their families wrote, 'We have nothing to eat, we are fed up with war, come back as soon as possible.'

B SOURCE

German women queuing for potato peelings in 1917.

C SOURCE

A comparison of industrial output by the Central Powers and the Allies in 1914. The figures are in millions of tons.

Allied Powers	Coal	Iron	Steel
Britain	292	11	6.5
France	40	5	3.5
United States	455	30	32
Central Powers			
Germany	277	15	14
Austria–Hungary	47	2	3

D SOURCE

German civilian deaths as a result of their poor diet.

1915	88,000
1916	120,000
1917	260,000
1918	294,000

E SOURCE

Richard Stumpf was a patriotic German who volunteered for the navy in 1912 and served on the battleship *Helgoland*. He made these comments in his diary towards the end of 1915 (quoted in *The Great War*, R Tames, 1984).

The officers have made no sacrifices at all so far . . . While we have to content ourselves to live on half rations of bread, they hold feasts . . . at which six or seven courses are served . . . All of us wish that the Helgoland would run over a mine so that the officers' quarters would be blown to pieces.

F SOURCE

This photograph shows some Germans taken prisoner towards the end of the war.

Questions

a What can you learn from Source A about the military and home fronts in Germany in 1918?

b Does Source D support the evidence of Sources A and B about how the war affected Germany's civilian population?

c How useful are Sources C and E as evidence of why Germany was defeated in 1918?

d 'Germany was defeated in 1918 because of the failure of Ludendorff's Spring Offensive.' Use the sources, and your own knowledge, to explain whether you agree with this view.

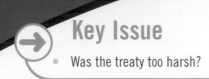

Key Issue

- Was the treaty too harsh?

'THE STAB IN THE BACK'?

After the failure of Germany's last military offensive of the First World War in March, 1918, the German army was gradually driven back by the Allied armies of Britain, France and the United States. One by one, Germany's allies surrendered until the Germans were left on their own against the Allies and agreed to an **armistice** or cease-fire on 11 November 1918. The Emperor or Kaiser of Germany, William II had abdicated, or given up the throne, two days earlier.

The German army had retreated slowly, without panicking and many of its soldiers didn't feel like a defeated army. Some were willing to go on fighting and blamed the new democratic government for 'stabbing the army in the back', for betraying the soldiers by agreeing to surrender. Adolf Hitler, who later became **dictator** of Germany, constantly repeated the idea of this 'stab in the back'. He called these democratic politicians who signed the armistice 'the November criminals'.

TERMS OF THE TREATY

Hitler became even more popular in Germany when he criticised the Treaty of Versailles. This was the treaty drawn up by David Lloyd George, the British Prime Minister, Georges Clemenceau for France, and Woodrow Wilson, the US President, which Germany had to sign. German opponents of the treaty, such as Hitler, called the treaty a 'Diktat' or dictated settlement in which they had no say. The **socialist** government, which took over from the Kaiser, was forced to take the blame for the defeat and the Treaty of Versailles which followed.

The treaty, from Germany's point of view, was harsh. First, the Germans were made to accept responsibility for starting the war, called Article 231 or the War Guilt clause. Then they had to pay for it. The Germans had to hand over territory to France and Poland and pay nearly £7 billion to Britain and France as **reparations** or compensation for the damage caused in the war. The German army was cut to just 100,000 men and there were to be no air force, submarines or tanks at all.

As a result of the treaty, Germany lost 13% of its land and six million German-speaking people were forced to become citizens of other countries, such as Czechoslovakia and Poland. All Germany's colonies were taken away and given to Britain and France to look after until they were ready to rule themselves. Harsh as it seemed, it wasn't as harsh as the terms which the French wanted but Wilson insisted on more lenient terms.

Some historians have criticised the treaty for punishing Germans so harshly that eventually they turned against their new government and democracy and chose Hitler instead. Some British economists at the time argued that Germany wouldn't be able to afford to pay the costs of the war because it had to hand over so many of its coal and iron-producing areas to other countries.

A SOURCE

A British army chaplain or priest, writing on 7 November 1918 – just four days before the war ended (quoted in *The Pity of War*, Niall Ferguson, 1998).

The Germans are fighting a clever defensive campaign . . . and have plenty of time to get back and form new machine-gun posts, which cause us heavy casualties as we advance . . . We all, except perhaps the senior officers who don't see anything of the fighting or the morale of the Germans, expect another six months of fighting.

B SOURCE

German troops returning to Berlin at the end of the war, cheered on by the civilian population.

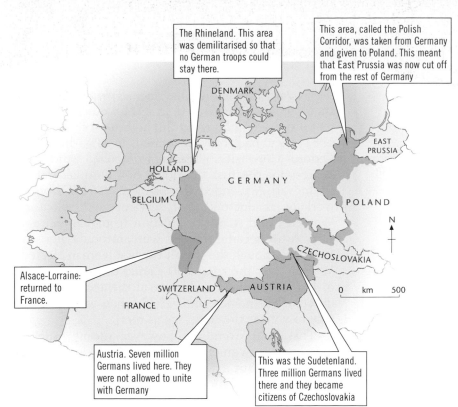

The Rhineland. This area was demilitarised so that no German troops could stay there.

This area, called the Polish Corridor, was taken from Germany and given to Poland. This meant that East Prussia was now cut off from the rest of Germany

DENMARK

EAST PRUSSIA

HOLLAND

GERMANY

BELGIUM

POLAND

N

CZECHOSLOVAKIA

Alsace-Lorraine: returned to France.

SWITZERLAND

AUSTRIA

0 km 500

FRANCE

Austria. Seven million Germans lived here. They were not allowed to unite with Germany

This was the Sudetenland. Three million Germans lived there and they became citizens of Czechoslovakia

Map of the Treaty of Versailles.

C SOURCE

General Ludendorff was one of the commanders of the German army on the Western Front. On 18 October 1918, he told the German government (quoted in *1914–1918*, J Winter and B Baggett, 1996):

The 41st Division absolutely refused to fight on August 8th [1918]; that was a black day in the history of Germany. The morale was bad at that time . . . the division had no potatoes. The attitude of the men from home was also bad. The new recruits lacked discipline. There were serious cases of the disobeying of orders.

D SOURCE

In his autobiograpy, *My Struggle*, written while he was in prison in 1924, Hitler described the November criminals.

I intensely loathed the whole gang of miserable party politicians who had betrayed the people . . . What counted with them was the possibility of fill-ing their own empty pockets. My opinion was that these people thoroughly deserved to be hanged because they were ready to allow . . . Germany to be defeated to benefit themselves.

F SOURCE

The German newspaper, *Deutsch Zeitung*, commenting on the Treaty of Versailles in June 1919:

Vengeance! German nation! Today the disgraceful Treaty is being signed. Do not forget it. The German people will, with unceasing work, press forward to reconquer the place among nations to which they are entitled. Then will come revenge for the shame of 1919.

E SOURCE

Revolutionary soldiers and civilians like these, who were opposed to the war, attempted to seize control of German towns and cities in the last months of 1918.

Questions

a What can you learn from Source A about the state of the German army in the later stages of the war?

b Does Source C support the evidence of Sources A and B about the morale of the German army in 1918?

c How useful are Sources D and E as evidence of conditions in Germany at the end of the war?

d 'Germany lost the war because its army was "stabbed in the back" by the politicians at home.' Use the sources, and your own knowledge, to explain whether you agree with this view.

Key Issue

- How far did the war really change the lives of women in Britain?

Germaine Greer, a feminist writer of the 1970s, suggested that women in the First World War were a bit like a captive bird whose cage is left open. They had a look outside but decided life was better inside the cage than out.

It is true that women seized the chance offered them by the war to show men (and themselves) what they were capable of doing. It is also true that many of these changes were only temporary and after the war, life for women returned to its traditional pattern. What that traditional pattern was depended very much on what class these women came from and whether they were married.

BEFORE 1914

Upper-class women did not work before the war and few worked after it. Working-class women, on the other hand, had to work to help keep their families. They worked before the war mostly in factories and in domestic service as maids. As many as 11% of all women worked as domestic servants before the war. The war gave the them chance to work in a greater variety of jobs but most of these new jobs were lost at the end of the war.

Fewer married women of all classes worked. In some cases, like teaching, they had to give up their jobs once they got married. But more working-class married women worked than women from other classes. In some parts of the country and in some occupations, such as the Lancashire textile mills, they were expected to carry on working after they married.

CHANGES AFTER THE WAR

Perhaps the most long-lasting change came about for middle-class women. Before the war middle-class women found job opportunities as teachers, nurses, telephonists, typists, and as sales assistants in up-market department stores. After the war there were better prospects for careers in the higher professions

(as lawyers, accountants and doctors) but this change should not be exaggerated. In 1911 women made up 6% of those employed in the higher professions. By 1951 they had only increased to 8%. In 1919, Oxford University allowed women to study for degrees for the first time. The Sex Disqualification (Removal) Act ended the ban on married women working as doctors, civil servants and solicitors. Women could stand for election to parliament and Lady Astor became the first woman to take her seat in 1919 – though she wasn't the first woman elected. Women over the age of 30 gained the right to vote in 1918 – but men could vote at the age of 21. This difference remained until 1928 when women were able to vote at the same age as men.

These improvements, however, meant little to working-class women. They probably welcomed the right to vote but it was the work of courageous pioneers like Marie Stopes who brought real benefits to their lives. In 1921 she opened Britain's first birth control clinic – but only for married women. Perhaps it could be said that it was only because of the changes in attitude brought about by the war that birth control could be discussed in the open for the first time.

'THE RIGHT TO SERVE'

When war first broke out the government was reluctant to allow women to do any of the jobs left vacant by the men who had gone to fight. Emmeline Pankhurst, a leading **suffragette**, campaigned vigorously with one of her daughters, Christabel, to have women more involved in the war effort. The Pankhursts organised 'The Right to Serve' procession in 1915 in which 60,000 women took part. The government was soon forced to change its mind and allow women into industry and other traditionally 'male' jobs. It was the only way to keep up production.

The number of women involved in the munitions industry, for example, increased from 200,000 in 1914 to 900,000 by 1918. Munitions work involved the manufacture of shells, weapons, and the handling of chemicals. It was dangerous and unhealthy work. These women were nick-named 'munitionettes' and, more seriously, 'canaries'. This was because the chemicals used turned their skin yellow. But the work, by women's standards, was well paid. A female industrial worker could expect to earn between three and five pounds a week – a huge sum compared to the two pounds a month for a domestic servant before the war. However, the improvement in women's wages had the disadvantage that fewer women kept their jobs after the war.

Women filled all sort of jobs – many of them dangerous. They worked in the shipyards and drove trams, buses and ambulances. 48,000 worked as labourers on the land in the Women's Land Army. These jobs proved women had the stamina and the skill to cope with tasks which people had thought only men could do. Farm work, though, was not a job women flocked to do. 210,000 vacancies remained unfilled.

HOW MUCH REALLY CHANGED DURING THE WAR?

Many think that the war created huge numbers of jobs for women in industry and that women took the places of their men who were at the front. But the statistics don't bear this out. Women made up only 31% of the new workers brought in to work in industry. In fact, more women – about 840,000 – found jobs outside industry in commerce and local government, for example. Nonetheless, about 700,000 women did play a vital role in the chemical, metal and munitions industries during the war.

Furthermore, few of these women wartime workers were new to paid work. As many as two-thirds were already in jobs before the war broke out, so the impact of the war on women workers should not be exaggerated. The vast majority of these workers already had jobs.

The skills which women acquired in industry during the war were not that new either. Few found work in jobs which were really new for women industrial workers. For example, shell-filling in the munitions industry, though dangerous, had already been done by women before the war. Generally speaking, as Jon Lawrence has written, women 'were not acquiring skills which would allow them to compete equally with male craftsmen after the war'.

THE POST-WAR 'CLEAR OUT'

In the first 18 months after the war some 600,000 women left their jobs – most of them voluntarily. They accepted that they had been filling in for their menfolk at the front. However, as many as half of the 'new' women workers taken on during the war still had their jobs as late as April 1920. But the economic slump of 1920–21 led to a widespread 'clear-out' of these women workers. In 1921 the percentage of the female population with a job was 31% – 1% less than in 1911. Only in commercial occupations did women get to keep the jobs they had in the war.

A NEW GENERATION

Despite this, women did emerge from the war with more confidence in their own abilities. The social and economic changes which women experienced during the war have been exaggerated. But the boost in their self-confidence – at least for middle-class women – could not easily be taken away. In the 1920s a new generation of mainly middle-class young women challenged traditional ideas about feminine behaviour. These women socialised with men on equal terms, smoked in public and drank in pubs. They went out with men without a chaperone (an elderly female relative, normally) to keep an eye on them. Their behaviour shocked many but these women were determined to stay on the outside of the 'cage' once they had tasted 'freedom'. Their daring allowed other women to make less dramatic but still important progress on the road to equality.

An official government photograph showing women dentists at work. This image of women involved in exciting new professions is the one often associated with women and the war. The reality for the vast majority was much more ordinary.

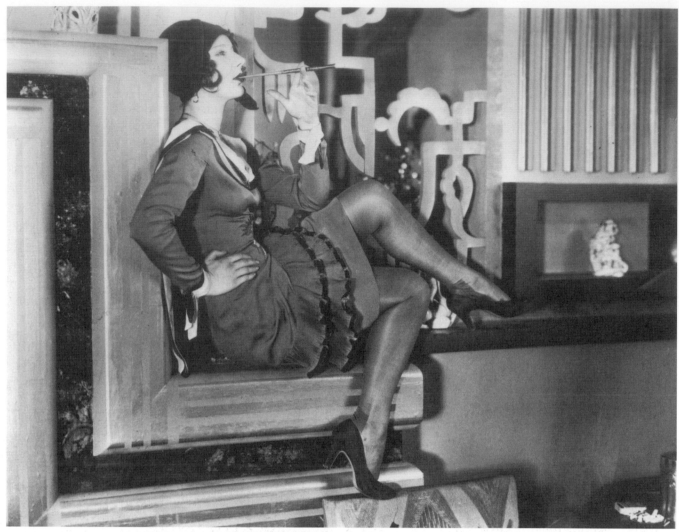

This photograph shows several features associated with the 1920s 'flapper'. She is wearing a short skirt, has a short, masculine haircut, and is smoking.

A SOURCE

The government encouraged paintings such as this one – titled *For King and Country* – which shows women munitions workers.

B SOURCE

One British woman, Daisy Collingwood, volunteered for work in a munitions factory at the age of 17. (From *Veterans*, R van Emden and S Humphries, 1998).

I loved the job. I'd lived such a sheltered life in the countryside that for me to get out and work with a lot of other people was just heaven. I didn't mind the danger, because I was given responsibility. I started on the night shift, something new in itself because I'd never stayed up all night in my life . . . Several times mum and dad tried to get me to leave, but I refused because for the first time I was living my own life.

C SOURCE

The official government caption for this Women's Land Army photograph was: 'A gleam of sunshine in the cowshed'.

D SOURCE

The historian, Trevor Wilson, on how the war affected the role of women as workers (from *The Myriad Faces of War*, T Wilson, 1996).

It had, of course, been the traditional view that if one sex or the other must go without work, then women should be the ones to do it. What is worth stressing is that the war had reinforced, rather than changed, this attitude.

Questions

a What can you learn from Source A about the role of women in the First World War?

b Use Source B and your own knowledge to explain why women were so keen to work in munitions factories.

c How useful is Source C as evidence about the role of women in the Women's Land Army?

d Is Source D a fair interpretation of how the war affected the position of women as workers? Use Source D and your own knowledge to answer the question.

How did the war affect the position of women in society?

Write a few sentences about each of the following:

- What life for women was like before the war
- How new opportunities came about during the war
- How women were treated after the war
- How long-lasting the changes were

THE ROSES OF NO MAN'S LAND

Women were quickly recruited into traditional nursing jobs once the war had broken out. 23,000 women served as qualified nurses, some of them on the Western Front, and they had to be at least 23-years-old before they would be allowed abroad. A further 80,000 volunteered to serve as nursing assistants in the Voluntary Aid Detachments (VADs) during the course of the war and about 8000 of these served abroad. Women in the VADs had only basic first aid training and were not paid, so they tended to come from wealthy families.

Many upper- and middle-class women came face to face with a side of life they had never experienced: dealing with the sick and wounded, the dying and the dead. These nurses and assistants became known as 'The Roses of No Man's Land', after the popular wartime song which celebrated their heroism and devotion to the men they cared for.

The work was hard and unpleasant, as one nurse recalled: 'The leg I was holding came off with a jerk and I sat down still clasping the foot. I stuffed the leg into the dressing pail beside the other arms and legs.'

EDITH CAVELL

Nursing, of course, was nothing new for women. But their closeness to the front did mean that they were exposed to physical danger from enemy action. Edith Cavell is an extreme example of how dangerous this role could be. She was a British nurse who found herself in a part of Belgium occupied by the Germans. She used her role as a nurse to help Allied soldiers stranded behind German lines get back to their own side.

This was obviously not a proper activity for a nurse but the German reaction was very severe. She was tried as a spy and executed in October 1915, despite pleas from neutral countries such as America. Among her final words was the rather puzzling statement that '**patriotism** is not enough'. This was another **propaganda** disaster for the Germans and she became a heroine in Britain. Incidents like this did a great deal to turn opinion in neutral countries – especially the United States – against Germany.

THE WOMEN'S SERVICES

At first the government resisted demands to allow women some role in the armed services as well as in nursing and industry. In 1917 it gave in. From the spring of 1917 there were many jobs in the armed services which women were able to do as well. 100,000 women served in the various sections of the armed services: the Women's Army Auxiliary Corps (WAAC), the Women's Royal Naval Service (WRNS) and the Women's Royal Air Force (WRAF). Here they took over the clerical and administrative jobs normally done by men. This allowed more men to go to the front.

Women in the WAAC were thought to be of a lower class than women in the other women's forces. They quickly gained a 'bad' reputation for sexual misconduct with the troops in France. But the 21 reported pregnancies among the 6000 WAAC personnel in France in 1918 suggest that these rumours were somewhat exaggerated. Nothing was said about the men involved in these affairs.

THE WOMEN'S LAND ARMY

The number of farm workers fell by 260,000 during the war as the men were conscripted or volunteered for the war. The government set up the Women's Land Army (WLA) in an attempt to persuade women to take their places. Maintaining food production was vital, especially because of the effects of the German U-boat campaign, and rationing had to be introduced mid-way through 1918. The response of women to the WLA was not enthusiastic. Working on farms was a hard, physical, and dirty job and, therefore, was considered unfeminine. Only 48,000 women volunteered for the WLA. As a result, men had to be brought back from the military front to work in the fields.

SOURCE

Alice Proctor was 19 when she went to France as a nurse in the VAD. This is how she described her training (from *The First World War*, M Brown, 2002).

How to stop bleeding with a tourniquet, and if it was a fracture you'd put a couple of broomsticks down the side of the leg and fasten them above and below the wound, and offer sweet tea for shock, which of course is quite wrong. And for burns, most astonishingly, to put flour on or bicarbonate of soda, which of course is quite wrong, you now just put it under the cold tap . . . You just picked it up as you went along.

B SOURCE

This British poster of 1917 (below) urged women to join the Women's Land Army.

C SOURCE

This British poster was published in 1915.

D SOURCE

The role of women in the First World War (adapted from *The Myriad Faces of War*, T Wilson, 1986).

Their role was to make it easier for men to join up and to make sure that any concern they might have for their families did not stop these men from offering their services, and possibly their lives, for their country.

Questions

a What can you learn from Source A about the training given to women in the VADs?

b Why was Source B distributed in Britain in 1917? Use Source B and your own knowledge to answer the question.

c How useful is Source C to an historian studying the role of women in the First World War? Use Source C and your own knowledge to answer the question.

d Is Source D a fair interpretation of the role played by women in the First World War? Use Source D and your own knowledge to answer the question.

20 CIVILIAN HARDSHIP

Key Issue

- How badly were civilians affected by the war?

RATIONING

The government came round to the idea of rationing reluctantly. It was afraid that rationing food would be very unpopular and that it would support rumours that the German U-boat campaign was bringing Britain to the point of defeat. In April 1917 German U-Boats sank over 370 ships belonging to Britain and other countries. One in every four merchant ships leaving a British port was being sunk. Losses on this scale would indeed bring Britain to the point of starvation.

To begin with, the government encouraged voluntary measures such as growing more food in private gardens or going without meat one day a week. It allowed bakers to save on flour by using flour substitutes instead. These included potatoes. People complained about the taste and the colour of the bread but at least it was never rationed.

In 1917 the government began to respond to the urgent problem of food shortages caused by the devastating German U-boat attacks on **merchant ships**. The price of a loaf of bread had more than doubled since 1914 and the government ordered a cut of 25% in its price. Controlling prices was certainly new for a British government but the introduction of rationing in 1918 was even more dramatic.

DO NOT FEED THE DOG

By mid-1918 meat, butter, sugar and margarine were all rationed. This was government control over people's lives on a vast scale – or at least, so it seemed. In fact, the rations laid down were generous and caused little hardship. But the queues disappeared and rationing was popular because people thought it was fairer.

Fines for breaches of the regulations were ferocious. One woman was fined £20 for feeding steak to her dog – and this was at a time when the average male wage was £2 a week. This fine, though, seemed lenient compared to that of £50 on a man who fed bread crusts to his pigs. Getting hold of an illegal extra ration book could lead to three months' imprisonment.

ENEMY ACTION

Rationing might have inconvenienced the population but it didn't threaten their lives – unlike attacks by German ships and aircraft. In December 1914, three German cruisers shelled three English coastal towns, causing 700 casualties and then in 1915 the Zeppelin airship raids began. Zeppelins were slow, full of flammable gas and carried a small bomb load. Blackout regulations were already in place before these air raids started. The Zeppelin raids in 1915 killed fewer than 150 people and had little effect on morale but they did increase popular hatred of the Germans as 'baby-killers'. There were attacks on businesses in Britain with German-sounding names, especially after the sinking of the *Lusitania*. Shops were looted and wrecked. King George V decided to abandon the British royal family's German name, Saxe-Coburg-Gotha, and chose Windsor instead.

By 1917 the Germans had changed from Zeppelins to aeroplanes as the most effective way to bomb British cities. These carried much bigger bomb loads and were used during the day. One raid on London killed 162 civilians, including 16 children in a school when a bomb penetrated three floors of a building before exploding in the cellar where they were sheltering. It was the worst raid of the war. During the course of the entire war about 2000 civilians were killed by enemy raids – rather fewer than the 66,000 British civilians who were to die in the Second World War.

A SOURCE

A British account by Sybil Morrison of a Zeppelin being shot down in September 1916 (from *The First World War*, M. Brown, 1991).

It was like a big cigar and all of the bag part had caught fire – the gas part. I mean it was roaring flames: blue, red, purple . . . And we knew there were about sixty people in it and they were being roasted to death . . . I was appalled to see the kind, good-hearted British people dancing about in the streets at the sight of sixty people being burned alive.

SOURCE

Food shortages in Britain. This poster was distributed in Britain by the government in 1917.

We risk our lives to bring you food. It's up to you not to waste it.

J.P.Beadle

"A Message from our Seamen"

D SOURCE

A modern historian on attitudes to the war (from *The Great War*, Josh Brooman, 1985).

By the end of 1916, however, civilians were losing their enthusiasm, for the war was changing their lives in ways they had never expected.

Questions

a **Look at Source A. Why did British civilians react in this way to the shooting down of a Zeppelin?**

b **Why did the British government issue posters like Source B in 1917? Use Source B and your own knowledge to answer the question.**

c **How useful is Source C to an historian studying the effect of German air raids on Britain?**

d **Is Source D an accurate interpretation of civilian attitudes to the war by the end of 1916? Use Source D and your own knowledge to answer the question.**

C SOURCE

British soldiers clearing up after the Zeppelin raid in September 1916.

21 STATE CONTROL

Before the Great War most politicians had accepted the view that governments should interfere as little as possible in peoples' lives and in the running of the economy. This is one reason why **conscription** was delayed until 1916. The government believed it should be up to the individual to decide whether he would fight for his country or not. The Great War changed this attitude. The government became involved in a wide range of areas such as industry, food supply and even pub opening hours.

The Liberal Party, led by Herbert Asquith, had been in power since 1905. The Liberals had already begun to change their minds about what the role of the state should be. The war – as is often the case – led to an even greater change in attitudes towards the role of government.

THE MUNITIONS SCANDAL

The government soon realised that vital industries, such as munitions, railways, mines and shipbuilding, all needed to be brought under state control. The public's mind was focused on this issue by the 'munitions scandal' of 1915 when the Commander-in-Chief of the British army, Sir John French, blamed the failure of a British offensive on a shortage of shells.

The immediate political effect of the scandal was that Asquith had to set up a **coalition government** with Liberal, Conservative and Labour politicians. He was also forced to create a Ministry of Munitions in May 1915 with the Liberal, Lloyd George, in charge. Lloyd George's policies led to an impressive increase in shell production. By mid-1916, a year's output of shells was now being produced in a couple of weeks – though it should also be pointed out that these shells were now needed by an army that was three times bigger than it had been in 1915 and against an enemy which was in much stronger defences.

STATE CONTROL

But the scandal also convinced Asquith that the privately run munitions industry was not delivering enough shells for the war effort. If this was true for munitions, then it was probably true for other industries too. It was accepted that the national interest in ensuring that these were run efficiently was more important than the private interests of their owners. Railways had already been taken over by the state but many other industries were now controlled indirectly by the government. The government did this by controlling the distribution of certain **raw materials**, such as sugar, meat, and wool, to factories.

DORA

The government increased its control over people's lives through a series of measures passed through the Defence of the Realm Act (DORA). Through DORA the government was able to take over factories and make them produce munitions. It cut pub opening hours to limit drunkenness. This had been a serious problem because pubs used to open at 5 a.m. and workers could stop off on their way to work. This was especially a worry in the munitions industry where accidents could have disastrous consequences.

The government also ordered beer to be watered down to make it less alcoholic. 'Treating' or the buying of rounds was also banned and it was enforced. One husband was prosecuted for buying his wife a drink. These measures were effective since convictions for drunkenness dropped to 10% of their 1914 numbers. The government also censored the press to make sure that it did not print stories damaging to morale or give away military information to the enemy. Bank holidays and even Guy Fawkes' night fireworks were cancelled.

A SOURCE

Lieutenant Rory Macleod, Royal Horse Artillery (from *1914–1918, Voices and Images of the Great War*, Lyn MacDonald, 1988).

*Owing to the heavy use of ammunition which seriously reduced our stocks and could not be replaced, we were cut to a ration of sixty shells per **battery** per week. The problem was whether to annoy the Germans by firing ten shells a day, or to save them up for a big attack on some important target.*

LEND YOUR
FIVE SHILLINGS
TO YOUR COUNTRY
AND

CRUSH
THE GERMANS

War Bonds: citizens were urged to lend money to the government to pay for the war. It is possible that the sum here was a regular one, rather than just a one-off contribution. Lending the government money was a patriotic act, since, if your country lost the war, you probably wouldn't get your money back.

B SOURCE

A cartoon in 'Punch' magazine, 1915. 'Labour' on the horse's collar refers to the workers, and 'capital' to businessmen.

DELIVERING THE GOODS.

C SOURCE

Letter to *The Times* newspaper, 17 June 1915. From an unnamed munitions worker (adapted from *1914–1918, Voices and Images of the Great War*, Lyn MacDonald, 1988).

Sir,
Will you allow me to point out one of the chief dif-ficulties at the moment and a solution? We have to deal, not so much with shirkers, but the real temp-tation among munitions workers to enlist in the army to save themselves from the silly sneers of their ignorant neighbours. Many valuable men are leaving my factory to join up, even though they were serving their country much better making munitions than as soldiers. Put them in the khaki uniform of soldiers. This would give them status and stop them feeling uncomfortable when dressed as civilians.

D SOURCE

Britain's response to the war (from *The Pity of War*, Niall Ferguson, 1998).

Led by the heroic figure of Lloyd George and his Ministry of Munitions, the British magnificently adapted to the demands of total war.

Questions

a What does Source A suggest about the supply of artillery shells?
b Why did 'Punch' magazine publish Source B in 1915? Use Source B and your own knowledge to answer the question.
c How useful is Source C to an historian studying 'the munitions scandal' of 1915?
d Is Source D an accurate interpretation of how Britain coped with the demands of the war? Use Source D and your own knowledge to answer the question.

22 A FAIRER, BETTER BRITAIN?

Key Issues

- How did the war affect the power of government?
- How did the war affect living standards?

WHAT CHANGED?

After the war the nationalised industries (those under **state control**) were returned to their private owners but an important principle had been established: the state had the duty to control some industries for the public good. The Labour government (1945–51) used this argument straight after the Second World War to justify its **nationalisation** policies. In the short-term, therefore, it seems that not much did change but in the long-term, the change in attitude was significant.

A 'LAND FIT FOR HEROES'?

People also expected a fairer and better Britain after the war. They wanted it to be the 'land fit for heroes' which Lloyd George had promised the returning troops. They wanted better education, better protection against the effects of sickness, unemployment and poor housing. But, on the other hand, people resented government interference in their daily lives, such as the restrictions on drinking, and the high taxes.

The standard tax rate had risen from six pence in every pound to 25 pence by 1918. How could the government bring about a 'land fit for heroes' without the higher taxes and more 'interference'? The government would have found it hard to pay for this new, fair and equal Britain, anyway. Taxes paid for only 11% of the cost of the war. The rest had largely been paid for by borrowing money from the public in the form of government war bonds. The money borrowed would be repaid by the government – with interest – after the war. As a result the government owed, at the end of the war, a staggering £7.4 billion – up from £650 million in 1914. On top of this, the government had the cost of widows' war pensions to pay.

HOW DID THE WAR AFFECT LIVING STANDARDS?

On average, wages rose by some 90% during the course of the war but the cost of living rose by 110%. This alone suggests that living standards fell by 20%. However, there were factors which meant that some people's living standards held up quite well. For one thing, rents were controlled during the war and were not allowed to increase above their August 1914 level. This meant that people had more money to spend because their rents stayed the same while their wages increased. This also helped to limit workers' demands for higher wages and reduced the number of strikes. Full employment and a lot of overtime also boosted earnings. This is particularly true for women who were now earning far more than they did before the war.

On the other hand, many **white collar workers**, such as teachers, got no pay increases at all and here living standards fell sharply. The departure of the main breadwinner in the family to the armed forces also caused real hardship where the loss of income could not be made up.

LLOYD GEORGE AND THE UNIONS

The government needed to ensure high levels of output in the factories to keep up with the war. To this end, Lloyd George believed that the influence of the trade unions in the workplace had to be reduced. He was particularly concerned with the issue of demarcation. This meant that only skilled workers could do certain jobs in certain industries – even if the job didn't really need much training. These demarcation rules kept skilled workers employed but slowed down production.

THE TREASURY AGREEMENT, MARCH 1915

Lloyd George arranged a conference with the unions in March 1915 to put an end to these practices. The result of this conference was the Treasury Agreement. Lloyd George insisted on the principle of 'dilution'. This meant that the unions would agree to skilled workers' jobs being done by semi-skilled or even unskilled workers.

Lloyd George was anxious to bring the unions into a sort of partnership rather than bully them. Therefore, the government made concessions too. Lloyd George promised the unions that these changes were only temporary. After the war, the old demarcation system would operate again. He also agreed that the workers doing skilled jobs would be paid the skilled rate even if they weren't skilled workers. This helped convince the skilled workers' unions that the government wasn't doing this to force down wages but only to provide more workers in key jobs.

Lloyd George also banned strikes in firms connected with the making of munitions. By the end of the war there were 6000 such firms. Workers could be fined for going on strike or simply missing work. Skilled workers could not leave for a job elsewhere without the permission of their employer. This was called the 'leaving certificate'. It was the most hated part of a law passed under the Munitions of War Act of July 1915. Any worker who left his or her job without this certificate would have to wait six weeks before starting another job. Few could afford such a long period without pay. The workers' leaders called this 'slavery'.

The official leaders of the trade unions were willing to make these compromises with Lloyd George. In exchange, Lloyd George promised to tax severely the very high profits made by some employers and to keep down the price of bread. The price of bread, for example, had more than doubled by 1917 from its 1914 price. Lloyd George ordered a 25% reduction in its price. However, some workers believed that the trade union leaders had given away too much. They decided that they would elect their own unofficial leaders to represent them. These were known as 'shop stewards'. One trade union, led by its shop stewards, decided to challenge the government.

THE CARROT ...

200,000 South Wales miners went on strike in 1915. Lloyd George declared that the strike was illegal (which it was not) and threatened to arrest the strikers. It was a daft threat, as he soon realised, and he settled the strike by giving in to their demands.

... AND THE STICK

There was also a strike in early 1916 in the shipyards of the river Clyde in Glasgow against the principle of dilution. A meeting between Lloyd George and 3000 shop stewards (unofficial union leaders) achieved nothing – except an accusation from the minister that 'there is German money up there'. Eventually he simply ordered the arrest of the strike leaders and fined any who remained on strike. Lloyd George got away with this because the strikers on the Clyde were all skilled workers and they did not have the support of other workers – unlike the South Wales miners – or the official trade union leaders.

These statistics refer to the number of days lost in British strikes during the First World War. Three million days lost in 1915 could be caused, for example, by one million workers going on strike for three days.

1914	9,900,000
1915	3,000,000
1916	2,400,000
1917	5,600,000
1918	5,900,000

CONSEQUENCES

The war did a great deal for both trade unions and the Labour Party. Unions before 1914 were not really an accepted part of British society. But the moderate and patriotic role played by the official trade union movement during the war convinced many that the unions were not out to create chaos and revolution. Membership between 1914 and 1919 doubled to eight million.

The Labour Party's reputation increased for much the same reason. Labour ministers in Lloyd George's **coalition government** showed that **socialists** could be responsible and patriotic. In 1924

This American war loans poster makes the direct link between money lent and bullets for the machine-gun. Americans lent $20.5 billion to their government in such loans.

Britain had its first Labour government. The Lloyd George Liberal government which ended in 1922 was the last one in Britain to date (2004). Labour replaced the Liberals as the main opposition to the Conservatives.

Immediately after the war, the mines were returned to their private owners. The miners demanded that the mines stay under state control and that the miners should run them. The war had proved, they claimed, that state control of industries worked for the benefit of all the people and not just their wealthy owners. The miners, though, would have to wait until 1947 for this.

feed the guns with WAR BONDS and help to end the War

Posters like this were used to persuade people to lend money to the government for the war effort.

Strikers outside the headquarters of the Amalgamated Society of Engineers, during the Woolwich Arsenal Strike.

Write an essay in answer to the following question: 'How far did the First World War change the lives of people in Britain?' You should include the following points:

- changes in the way government controlled people's individual lives, such as *conscription*, rationing, censorship
- changes in the status and role of women
- changes in the way government controlled the economy, for example state control of industries; trade unions.

In each paragraph, link what you write back to the question, so that you are not just describing how the war affected people but also whether it changed their lives or the government's policy.

Set your answer out like this:

Introduction
Briefly explain the areas or topics you are going to write about.

Paragraph 1
People's attitudes to the role of government before the war; how the war changed individual lives.

Paragraph 2
What life was like for women before the war; changes to the status and role of women during the war; what happened after the war.

Paragraph 3
The politician's views about what powers government should have over the economy; changes in the economy during the war; policies of later governments.

Conclusion
It is important to make clear what your judgement is about the *extent* of these changes. Were they long-lasting or just short-term changes which didn't last beyond the war? Did the changes apply more to one area than another?

The use of the correct *technique* is the key to success in source evaluation papers and this counts for much more than the application of knowledge. The best way to improve this technique, as for any skill, is practice.

EDEXCEL

The sources on which these examples are based are on pages 10–13.

(a) *What can you learn from Source A about the battle of Mons? (4 marks)*

TECHNIQUE

- To get more than 2 marks for this question you must read between the lines and make an inference, i.e. write something that the source *suggests* or *implies*.
- A couple of inferences with some explanation will be enough for 4 marks.
- It is a good idea to start your answer with the same phrase each time, i.e 'Source A suggests . . .' or 'Source A implies . . .'
- Example: *'Source A implies that the German commanders didn't care that much about the lives of their men and that sticking to their plan was more important. It also suggests that the British forces were not really ready for this battle ("after taking up positions as best they could") and that this and their lack of numbers could have led to their defeat.'*

(b) *Does Source C support the evidence of Sources A and B about the Battle of Mons? (6 marks)*

TECHNIQUE

- It is essential (for 5/6 marks) to discuss the extent to which the sources agree. Do this in a concluding sentence or sentences.
- Do not compare Source A with B. You will get no credit for this.
- Do not comment on whether the sources are reliable or who wrote them. You will get no credit for this.
- Compare Source C with A, then C with B. Do not compare C with A and B together.
- Example: *'Source C states that the British were "in danger of finding themselves alone" and this is sup-*

ported by A where it refers to them being in danger of being surrounded. However, there is no reference in A to the French withdrawing or that the British retreated. There isn't that much in Source B which supports C. B talks about how the British were shooting down the Germans without much trouble and there is nothing in C about this. On the other hand, B does refer to the British being shoved "out of the field eventually" and this confirms the point about the British having to retreat in C. On balance, C is mostly supported by A and, to a lesser extent, by B'.

- Note the use of appropriate connectives: 'However', 'On the other hand', 'On balance'.

(c) *How useful are Sources D and E as evidence of the reasons for the failure of the Schlieffen Plan? (8 marks)*

TECHNIQUE

- It is essential in this question to write about the **type, provenance** *or purpose* of the sources if you are to get more than 6 marks but you don't have to comment on all three.
- All of the sources in this question will be useful for something.
- A source is still useful, even if it isn't reliable.
- Example, writing about Source D you could say: *'Source D is potentially very useful in explaining the reasons for the failure of the Schlieffen Plan since it tells us that the fire-power of each machine-gun was the same as sixty men with rifles. These would have killed many of the Germans as they attacked. On the other hand, the provenance of the source doesn't tell us how many of these weapons the BEF had in 1914. If it was only a few, they wouldn't have made that much difference.'*

(d) *'The Schlieffen Plan failed because of the British role at the Battle of Mons.' Use the sources, and your own knowledge, to explain whether you agree with this view. (12 marks)*

TECHNIQUE

- It is not a good idea to go through the sources one by one, from A to F.
- Group the sources into those which support the point of view of the question and those which do not. Then discuss them.
- You don't have to comment on all the sources to get high marks but three is a minimum.
- You must use both the sources and your own knowledge; otherwise you will lose half the marks available.
- You must finish with a conclusion which makes clear what your judgement of the question is.

There isn't a right or wrong answer to this question – you just need to support it with appropriate use of the evidence.

- Example: 'In conclusion, the sources do not seem to support the view of the question. Source B comes closest to supporting this argument but A and C both suggest that the British were only able to slow the German advance a little. Perhaps, as E indicates, the Russians played a more important role because they forced the Germans to weaken the Northern Army invading Belgium.'

AQA

The sources on which these examples are based are on pages 2–3.

(a) *What does Source A tell us about the sort of men who volunteered to fight in 1914? (3 marks)*

TECHNIQUE

- This is a straightforward question and you need only provide three short sentences, each containing a relevant piece of information from the source or making an inference, i.e. writing something the source suggests or implies.
- You will get no credit for adding knowledge of your own.
- Do not waste time by writing too much here.
- Example: '*Source A tells us that some of the men who volunteered were criminals. One had been arrested for looting German shops. Looters were given the choice of serving their sentences or joining up.'*
- Or you could make an inference: '*Source A suggests that not all the men who joined the army in 1914 were full of **patriotism**. Some joined up to escape a prison sentence rather than because of a sense of duty.'*

(b) *Use Source B and your own knowledge to explain why men volunteered for the army in the early years of the war. (6 marks)*

TECHNIQUE

- You must use both the source and some own knowledge to get more than two marks.
- You must also provide more than one reason for marks in the higher levels.
- Comment on the purpose of the source and its historical context.
- Example: '*This poster appeals to the patriotic feelings and sense of duty which many Britons felt in 1914 and 1915. These feelings led 750,000 men to volunteer in the first two months. The poster suggests that men who didn't volunteer were not doing their duty and many did join up out of a sense of guilt. Others enlisted to escape from boring jobs or poverty or because they were enraged by the atrocities Germans were said to be committing in Belgium.'*

(c) *How useful is Source C as evidence of the British public's reaction to the outbreak of war? Use Source C and your own knowledge to answer this question. (8 marks)*

TECHNIQUE

- You need to make use of the provenance of the source to score top marks and discuss its purpose.
- You should also test its usefulness by comparing it with your own knowledge.
- Don't confuse usefulness with reliability – a source is still useful even if it isn't reliable.
- Example: '*We don't know for certain whether this photograph was published during the war since the provenance doesn't tell us, and this limits its usefulness. But it probably was since it shows popular support for both the war and the King and Queen and this is what the government wanted. While it is possible that this photograph wasn't typical of the way the people felt about the war, what we know about the response to enlist suggests it was. Over 750,000 men volunteered for the armed forces in the first two months of the war and this indicates a great deal of enthusiasm for the war. There is, therefore, no reason to doubt the reliability of the source and this adds to its usefulness.'*

(d) *Is Source D a fair interpretation of why men volunteered for the army in the First World War? Use Source D and your own knowledge to answer the question. (8 marks)*

TECHNIQUE

- Once again, it is important to discuss the provenance of the source and to provide detailed own knowledge to help decide how fair or accurate the interpretation is.
- You must also consider the type of source it is and its content
- Ask yourself whether the content is typical of what you already know about the event. If it is, then it is more likely to be accurate.
- Example: '*The reasons given in the source are those of Robert Burns and it is possible that his reasons were not shared by many. On the other hand, it is clear that the idea that the war would be 'over by Christmas' was widely believed. The excitement which swept Burns along to join up affected tens of thousands like him. His decision to join up to be with 'a lot of lads' ties in with what we know about peer group pressure and the attraction of being in a 'Pals battalion.' In addition, we have no reason to suspect that he might not be telling the truth – he would have no reason to mislead the interviewer more than eighty years after the event'.*
- Note the use of appropriate connectives: '*On the other hand*', '*In addition*'.

GLOSSARY

absolutist – someone who refuses to undertake any activity associated with war (even non-combatant duties)

armistice – an agreement between two sides in a war to stop fighting

battery – a group of four artillery guns

blockade – blocking off a place by surrounding it with troops or ships so that no supplies can get in

censorship – the process of removing information from newspapers, films, books and so on, in order to keep it secret from the public

coalition government – a government formed by two or more parties working together

conscription – a law that requires people to serve in the armed forces

division – an army unit consisting of about 15,000 troops

hydrophone – an underwater listening device used to locate submarines

merchant ships – ships which carry supplies and are not equipped for war

military service – service in one of the armed forces i.e. army, navy or air force

mobilisation – getting an army ready to fight

mutiny – refusal to obey the orders of a higher-ranked soldier, such as an officer

nationalisation – state ownership, usually of an industry like shipbuilding

No Man's Land – the land between opposing trenches which neither side controls

pacifist – someone who is opposed to war for moral, religious or political reasons and refuses to fight but may carry out non-combatant duties, such as stretcher bearer

patriotism – support for your country, especially against its enemies

propaganda – persuading people to believe certain ideas and behave in a certain way; sometimes involves telling lies

provenance – where a source comes from. Who wrote it? When? Who was intended to read it? What role did the writer have?

raw materials – materials which occur naturally, such as coal, iron and oil, and which are then used to manufacture something else

reconnaissance – checking an enemy activity, often by using aircraft

recruiting sergeant – a soldier whose job is to encourage men to enlist

regimental aid post – place where basic medical treatment is given

reparations – compensation for damage caused in war

saps – short trenches leading off from the main trench system

socialist – someone who believes that the government should run the country for the benefit of the working people

state control – a policy which involves the government or state taking control of one or more industries

suffragette – campaigner for the right of women to vote

supply lines – ways in which armies are kept supplied with food and ammunition etc.

white collar workers – employees who work in an office or in a profession, such as teaching

INDEX

The publishers would like to thank the following individuals, institutions and companies for permission to reproduce copyright illustrations in this book:
Imperial War Museum, London: pp 2, 6, 7, 9, 10, 12 16, 19 (top and bottom), 23 (top and bottom), 28, 29, 33 (bottom), 36, 41 (top), 43 (right), 44, 47, 48 (bottom), 49, 51 (left and right), 53 (bottom); © Michael St. Maur Sheil/CORBIS: p 13; John Singer Sargent *Gassed*, 1918/ ©IWM # 1460: p 33 (top); The Art Archive: p3; Australian War Memorial: p 4; Punch: pp 5, 55 (right); The Art Archive/ Australian War Memorial: p 25; AKG Images: pp 31 (left), 45; Mary Evans Picture Library: p 35; The Art Archive/ Imperial War Museum: p 41 (bottom); Ullstein Bild Berlin: p 43 (left); Hulton Archive/ Getty Images: pp 48 (top), 59; The Art Archive/ Imperial War Museum/ Eileen Tweedy: p 58.

Text acknowledgements.
Abacus for the extract from *The Bloody Game* edited by P Fussell (1991); Andromeda Oxford Ltd for extracts from *The Experience of World War I* by J M Winter (1988); Arnold for the extract from *Octobrists to Bolsheviks* by M McCauley (1984); BBC Books for the extracts from *1914-1918* by J Winter and B Baggett (1996); BBC TV for material from *Time Watch* (1996); Collins for material from *People's Century* by G Hodgson (1995); Constable and Robinson Ltd for the extract from *Nurse at the Russian Front* by F Farmborough (1974); Croom Helm Ltd for extracts from *Eye in Deep Hell* by J Ellis (1979); extracts from *Forgotten Voices of the Great War* by Max Arthur published by Ebury, used by permission of The Random House Group Limited; Granada Publishing for the extract from *The War in the Trenches* by A Lloyd (1976); R Hale Ltd for extracts from *The War Walk* by N Jones (1983); Harrap for the extract from *I Saw Them Die* by S Millard (1936); Heinemann Publishers for the concept of 'crossing the T' from *History and Teaching and Historical Understanding* by A K Dickinson and P J Lee; Leo Cooper for extracts from *The Price of Pity* by M Stephen (1996) and *Veterans* by R van Emden and S Humphries (1998); Longman for the extract from *The Great War* by J Brooman (1985); Pan Books for the extracts from *The Firsy World War* by M Brown (2002) and *The Somme* by M Brown (1996); Penguin for extracts from *1914-1918 Voices and Images of the Great War* by L MacDonald (1988), *Death's Men* by D Winter (1979), *Dictionary of Modern History* by D Townson (1998), *The First Day of the Somme* by M Middlebrook (1971) and *The Pity of War* by N Ferguson (1998); Polity Press for the extracts from *The Myriad Faces of War* by T Wilson (1986); Sidgwick and Jackson for extracts from *The Imperial War Museum Book of the First World War* by M Brown (1991); SPA books for the extract from *Tank Warfare* by F Mitchell (1933); the illustration showing 'why soldiers feared going over the top' redrawn, with permission, from an illustration taken from *Key History for Key Stage 3: The Twentieth-Century World* (Stanley Thornes (Publishers) Ltd, 1995); Wellfleet Press for the extract from *The Poster in History* by M Gallo (1989).

The publishers will be glad to make suitable arrangements with any copyright holders whom it has not been possible to contact.

Artwork on pp 2, 9, 12, 25, 27, 39 by Martin Sanders (Beehive Illustration).

Orders: please contact Bookpoint Ltd, 130 Milton Park, Abingdon, Oxon OX14 4SB. Telephone: (44) 01235 827720. Fax: (44) 01235 400454. Lines are open from 9.00 – 6.00, Monday to Saturday, with a 24-hour message answering service. You can also order through our website www.hodderheadline.co.uk.

British Library Cataloguing in Publication Data
A catalogue record for this title is available from the British Library

ISBN 0 340 814 19 5

First Published 2004
Impression number 10 9 8 7 6 5 4 3 2 1
Year   2010 2009 2008 2007 2006 2005 2004

Cover photo shows a detail from *Dressing the Wounded During a Gas Attack* by Austin O Spare. Courtesy of The Imperial War Museum.

Typeset by Fakenham Photosetting Limited, Fakenham, Norfolk.
Printed in Dubai for Hodder & Stoughton Educational, a division of Hodder Headline, 338 Euston Road, London NW1 3BH.